'In *How to Be (Un)Successful*, Pete Portal is honest, raw and brilliant. He redefines or rather properly defines the metrics of kingdom fruitfulness. In a world of mega everything, this book is a refreshing reminder of what it looks like to walk in the joy of working out the call of God in your life. In our current culture of self-obsessed activism and personal rights, Pete does a masterful job of calling us deeply into Jesus and finding our true expression in and through him. This is no self-help book. It is not a manual. It is a theologically rich and experiential framework, guiding us into true purpose and fulfilment with all its highs and lows. Read it. It is to be digested and incarnated!'

Dr Katia and Julian Adams, founding pastors of The Table Boston, authors (respectively) of *Equal: What the Bible says about women, men, and authority* and *Terra Nova: Fulfilling your call to redeem the earth and make all things new*

'In this provocative book, Pete casts a vision. His vision is of a world where what we profess to believe and the lives we actually live are brought together in congruence. Addressing the worlds of faith and culture with astute analysis and prophetic incisiveness, Pete offers a timely and hope-filled clarion call for today's generation to reconsider how to live lives of true influence.'

Ken Costa, chairman, Leadership College, London

'Pete Portal offers a refreshing critique of contemporary notions of success, inviting readers into an (un)success "in the world" that is only possible when we embrace as success "not of this world". He offers a rich alternative vision of Jesus-inspired success, born of years of painful struggle living out the gospel in the heart of the impoverished South African township of Manenberg. Pete's vision is born out of his location in a setting of poverty, rampant addiction and gang violence, where dimensions of Christian faith cannot remain separated: contemplation inspires action, Holy Spirit revivalism engenders social justice activism, and power joins compassion. This book feeds a growing hunger like few others, threatening to incite a renewal movement deep enough to warm up hearts growing cold, and positively contagious enough to reach and recruit many to join Jesus and choose the kingdom of God as the best alternative nov

Bob Ekblad, co-founder and director of Seminary, and author of *Reading the Bible*

T0017620

'Whenever I look at the actual state of things (the world, the Church, the guy in the mirror), I'm reminded of how desperately I need people such as Pete Portal who can speak from personal experience with prophetic clarity about a better way to live, pray and define success. *How to Be (Un)Successful* is an invitation to follow the call of Christ by pursuing depth over breadth, building real relationships, and engaging faithfully with the culture around me. I remember flying into Cape Town on my way to stay with Pete and Sarah in Manenberg once, and the immigration officer asked where I was heading. I told her and suddenly she bellowed "No! You don't want to go there." A little desperately I told her I did, and this time she asked why. I smiled my widest smile and said "Because I've heard that Jesus lives there!" At this she roared with laughter, ceremonially stamped my passport, and welcomed me to South Africa. *How to Be (Un)Successful* carries the authority of someone who walks the talk, and I particularly appreciated the honest way in which Pete shares his struggles. It's as challenging as its title implies (thank God for that), but it's also inspiring, beguiling and brimming with hope.'
Pete Greig, 24-7 Prayer International and Emmaus Rd, England

'Pete's own lived faith authenticates and validates the challenging message he brings in this book. His writing stirs, encourages and inspires us in equal measure on our journey with Jesus, and enables us to use different metrics in working out what constitutes a life well lived.'
Simon Guillebaud, author and founder of Great Lakes Outreach Burundi

'Pete Portal has always written from the raw reality of where he lives and those he serves – here he adds, not just descriptions of complexity, but a love-shaped certainty of how to face our uncomfortable selves. I especially paused on the paragraphs about pain. Everything in our world now seeks to eradicate pain – distraction, medication, denial – but it is the echo of an opportunity to grow empathy and to embrace pressure. Because he who is the way, the truth and the life faced pain, I can now be free to be healed and hold hope in my heart. What I love about Pete's writing is its truth and experience and perspective and possibilities and wonder – a fountain of refreshing thinking.'
Lord Dr Michael Hastings CBE, Professor of Leadership, Huntsman Business School

'I love reading about heroes of the faith who have lived before us and changed the world, but I find it absolutely incredible when you get the privilege of meeting someone who is daring to live a life of such radical faith that they are changing the world right now. Pete Portal is one of those people I have had the honour of knowing. I have been so inspired and challenged by the way Pete has given his life to see heaven come to earth and captives set free. It is an honour to call him a friend and I am very excited about this new book.'
Jonathan Helser, songwriter and founder of The 18 Inch Journey

'When the Church loses confidence in its mission, story and central convictions, secular narratives begin to masquerade as kingdom narratives. These are then embraced by the Church, which then inevitably begins to lose it spiritual vibrancy and potency. We desperately need a wake-up call, which is why I love listening to Pete Portal preach and why I love his new book *How to Be (Un)successful*. Pete has been raised up as a prophet for such a time as this. He offers a diagnosis for the cultural moment we find ourselves in, invites us on a journey of detoxing from the ways of the world that have damaged our souls, and leads us back to the person, example and ministry of Jesus, where a whole new vision for life is presented. This is the kind of book you want to place in the hand of every follower of Jesus disillusioned by the world, or even the Church, but desperate to rediscover the upside-down way of the kingdom.'
Pete Hughes, Lead Pastor, KXC, London, and author of *All Things New: Joining God's story of re-creation*

'Great leaders ask great questions. This book raises excellent questions, bringing significant insights and fuel for all disciples seeking to live a kingdom life in the culture and world we inhabit. Much like Pete, this book is reflective, punchy, prophetic and engaging.'
Tim Hughes, Senior Pastor, Gas Street Church

'In this book, you will find yourself rethinking how you have lived your life and asking bigger questions about how to be human in this world. Pete takes you on a necessary journey of reflecting on the life of Jesus and the vast difference between it and how we live our lives now. This book is an invitation to move closer and closer to being someone you were designed to be. Let us say yes to this invitation!'
Eric Johnson, co-founder and Lead Pastor of Studio Greenville

'In a culture of hyper noise, clickbait and chasing after the next thing, *How to Be (Un)Successful* offers a refreshing insight into real-life big questions. This unnerving and holy book disturbed me, encouraging me to dig deeper, to unlearn merely inherited theology and truly pour into new wineskins. Beautifully told as a story of Manenberg, this could equally be a story about South Africa and the continent.

'Pete offers powerful and honest reflections on immersion, baptism in a community, and life with addicts of Church and addicts of drugs. Perhaps the shifts in the book are the prophetic insights for those brave enough not to consume but to commune – truly to immerse themselves in mission that changes both the messenger and the "beneficiary".

'In a world that is busy, confusing, noisy and discriminating, this book offers a different kind of solace, amid chaos, violence and failures of ministry. It provides a guide to walking with the broken and breaking Jesus – not the Jesus whom culture has produced, but the transforming one, the one who lets us transform. The South African Church needs new communion elements which realise that the body of Christ must be broken in order to be transformative to its audience. To be (un)successful is to lay down our lives for the ideals of the Gospels, pick up our cross and follow him. I recommend this book for those who want to dig deeper, (un)learn and walk further along in the footsteps of Jesus Christ, who is sorely missed in much of the religion and jargon we see today.'
Mmusi Maimane, Leader, Build One South Africa

'An appealing account by Pete, which I encourage all to read.'
The Most Revd Dr Thabo Makgoba, Archbishop of Cape Town

'Actions speak louder than words. Or, as Jesus taught us, "By their fruits ye shall know them" (Matthew 7.20 KJV). Pete Portal is a man who follows the Lord, and his fruits are bountiful. And by those fruits his words have earned our attention.'
Winston Marshall, musician and contributor to *The Spectator*

'Pete's is a voice I trust. He hasn't just developed deep and beautiful theology – he lives a life that keeps his heart breaking open. He is a witness to the glory of God, moving through grit, grime and grace. An earthy, downward trajectory that leads to the kingdom of God. This book is going to help you to find your way there.'

Danielle Strickland, author, speaker and activist

'With characteristic humility and ingenuousness, Pete Portal offers an extended meditation on the full dimensions of Jesus' words, "Whoever wants to save their life will lose it, but whoever loses their life for me and for the gospel will save it" (Mark 8.35). In the process, he never takes his eyes off the practical choices, sacrifices and implications of following Jesus, and never forgets that the best model for following Jesus is Jesus himself. The best teachers are able to say, "Do what I do." Pete Portal's witness in the humble surroundings of Manenberg, South Africa, is the best commendation of the profound truths this book explores.'

Sam Wells, Vicar of St Martin-in-the-Fields and Visiting Professor of Christian Ethics, King's College London

Pete Portal helps to lead Tree of Life, a church in Manenberg running ministries among the vulnerable and marginalised, and dedicated to living out Jesus' love as spiritual community. He is also on the board of 24-7 Prayer South Africa and spends much of his time growing relationships and networks across racial and socio-economic divides.

HOW TO BE (UN)SUCCESSFUL

An unlikely guide to human flourishing

Pete Portal

FORM

First published in Great Britain in 2023

Form
c/o SPCK
Studio 101
The Record Hall
16–16A Baldwin's Gardens
London EC1N 7RJ
www.spck.org.uk

British Library Cataloguing-in-Publication Data
A catalogue record for this book is available from the British Library

ISBN 978–0–281–08817–1
eBook ISBN 978–0–281–08818–8

1 3 5 7 9 10 8 6 4 2

Typeset by Fakenham Prepress Solutions, Fakenham, Norfolk NR21 8NL
First printed in Great Britain by Clays Ltd

eBook by Fakenham Prepress Solutions, Fakenham, Norfolk NR21 8NL

Produced on paper from sustainable sources

For Sarah,
You are so beautifully (un)successful.
Thank you for teaching me.

'Three things are necessary for the salvation of man: to know what he ought to believe; to know what he ought to desire; and to know what he ought to do.'
(Thomas Aquinas, *Two Precepts of Charity*, 1273)

Contents

Acknowledgements   xii
Foreword   xiii

Introduction   1

1 Success is ... Following God's calling over good ideas   12
   How God wants to mess you up and waste your life

2 Success is ... Pursuing relationship over relevance   32
   On friendship with God and people

3 Success is ... Growing in depth over volume   62
   Why influence looks different from what we've been told

4 Success is ... Transforming over transferring   88
   What will you do with your pain?

5 Success is ... Being a faithful presence in the culture wars   110
   Why the kingdom is inherently political

6 Success is ... Living in power and participation   137
   On suffering and the supernatural

Notes   163

Acknowledgements

Elizabeth Neep – for your belief in and vision for this book.

The SPCK and 24-7 Prayer teams – for the considerable work and support that went into this.

Jake – for coming up with the title, and some sweet slides.

Bill and Joyce, Penny and Richard – for letting me use your space to write.

Clare, Leon, Cynth and Sarah – for trusting me with Fridays.

Foreword

The Christian mystic Thomas Merton once said,

> If you write for God you will reach many men and bring them joy. If you write for men – you may make some money and you may give someone a little joy and you may make a noise in the world, for a little while.[1]

I agree, and I think he missed something. Who am I to add to Merton? But here it goes anyway: if you write for God you will disrupt many men and women, but it'll be the best kind of disruption, like being awakened by the bumps of a flight landing on the runway – it's jarring for a moment, followed by the delightful surprise that you've reached your destination. That's how I'd characterize Pete Portal's writing – delightfully disrupting, jarring in a way that awakens me to my true destination.

Every summer, I make a pilgrimage back to the rural American South of my childhood, travelling highways to hug family members and reminisce about another year passed in a blur. Along those highway miles, I occasionally pass billboards or church signs reading, 'Where Will You Spend Eternity?' or the more aggressive, 'Turn or Burn!' These messages, a relic of a church era gone by everywhere in the modern West *except* the rural American South, hold within them a great irony. They do not make me think of Jesus but of the human authors behind the billboard message.

I count Pete Portal a friend. I've laughed with him over dinner, prayed with him through tears, listened to his most honest and unfiltered rants, and heard his vulnerable confessions, and he mine. I can tell you what he'd readily admit: he is not a perfect man with perfect motives. He is writing for God in spite of himself, fighting the urge with each strike of the key to write for humankind, making nothing more than noise, for a little while.

And because Pete is writing for God, I have only to issue a warning and an invitation as you embark on the journey through these pages.

I'm a 'bad news first' kind of guy, so we might as well start with the warning: the book you're about to read – equal parts Hudson Taylor-esque missionary tales, Mary Karr confessional memoir and John the Baptist prophetic echo from the wilderness – is, like all words written for God, disruptive. But disruptive in a way that awakens you to the delight that you've been sleepily carried hundreds of miles nearer your soul's true destination.

And, while framing it as bad news, I honestly believe that to be the highest compliment I could offer this (or any other) book. It reads not unlike the red-letter words of Jesus in the Gospels – ever-inspiring, deeply comforting and occasionally quite disrupting. But if you want to help anyone else in any real way, if you write to enliven the soul rather than massage the ego, you're going to have to be all right with disruption, and Pete, whether vulnerably trembling or self-assured I don't know, has made his peace with disruption and served it up to you and me right alongside the inspiration and comfort. And for that, I'm grateful as a reader, proud as his friend, and spurred on as his brother in the faith.

Do not read this book if you seek only to stay asleep, only to keep marching drowsily forward apart from any startling disruption. Because to crack this binding and peruse these pages is an exercise in disruption of the most delightful variety.

At this point, I'm guessing the bad news makes the good news evident: the disruption is the best part. Like an acquired taste you mature into as you inch towards adulthood, what is first bitter grows into delicacy for anyone serious about following Jesus over the long haul. Our souls acquire a taste for conviction and self-reflection, and a resilience to return to the narrow way we never tire of wandering from.

It seems to me that the very words of Jesus that disrupted most profoundly at first, for those who stay by him, revealed the most profound truths in the end. Take, for instance, his words in John 6, after feeding the five thousand. 'Very truly I tell you, unless you eat the flesh of the Son of Man and drink his blood, you have no life in you' (John 6:53). With those few words, Jesus' most popular moment became his undoing, by modern measures of success at least. Most of his followers left him, and even the Twelve, who stayed, did so in spite of the bitter aftertaste his disturbing words left in their mouths after such a satisfying lunch.

It was Peter who said it, 'Lord, to whom shall we go? You have the words of eternal life' (John 6:68). Peter, and the eleven others, sure he and he alone could guide their souls, even if there were stretches of the journey that felt turbulent, welcomed the disruption. And so it was Peter and the others who sat with Jesus at the table we've never stopped gathering around, to receive the broken bread we continue to receive in remembrance of him, and listen to that same disruptive voice say, 'Take and eat; this is my body' (Matthew 26:26). The disruption satisfied their souls in a way that even the miraculous meal among the masses on the hillside couldn't. And in the hours that followed, they watched Jesus lead the most (un)successful victory in human history.

So I guess you could browse the shelves at your local Christian bookstore. They'll be full of words that are attempting to import the way of Jesus into the pursuits of success we've swallowed whole and think we can carry with us all the way to abundant life. Those books would certainly comfort and inspire you. They'll probably make more noise than this one, to be honest ... for a little while.

But *this* is not *that*.

This book will woo you, startle you and arrest you. It'll provoke you, wrestle you to the ground, keep you up at night, widen your sleepy eyes and, at the end of it all, you'll thank it for that. I did.

Tyler Staton, author of *Praying Like Monks, Living Like Fools* and *Searching for Enough*, Lead Pastor, Bridgetown Church, and National Director, 24-7 Prayer USA

Introduction

To be human is to be animated and oriented by some vision of
the good life, some picture of what we think counts as 'flourishing.' And we *want* that. We crave it. We desire it … We are
oriented by our longings, directed by our desires.
(James K. A. Smith[1])

In a world where success is the measure and justification of
all things the figure of Him who was sentenced and crucified
remains a stranger and is at best the object of pity. The world
will allow itself to be subdued only by success.
(Dietrich Bonhoeffer[2])

You probably want to be a success.

Chances are that's why you picked up this book.

And that's all right – it's a very reasonable thing to desire.

The questions 'Am I successful?' or 'What is success?' are deeply
significant and to ask such questions is a normal part of the
human experience. The yearning for a life of purpose, as elusive as
it can seem, is felt acutely by the majority of those who have ever
lived – certainly by more than might admit it. (Those feelings of
inadequacy you experience may be more common than you think.)
And now more than ever it is understandable that you may feel
you are not particularly successful, or not successful *enough*. We
are assaulted by a combination of capitalism and consumerism,
social media and cancel culture, polarised ideologies and virtue

signalling, the wounds of our parents passed down and just plain old original sin – all of which can amalgamate into producing some pretty angsty, pressure-driven people.

It's not just you; I'm pretty sure we all have a bit of a problem with success (the word itself is so subjective), and our idea of it can often be fuelled by wounds rather than vision, romanticised projections rather than reality. Because we are all somewhat flawed, any worldly contribution we try to make can get precariously entangled with a me-fixated narcissism on a fairly regular basis.

Most of us know that being successful is not simply about money, looks, large numbers or power. That's just a caricature to which very few reasonable people actually subscribe, right?

Well, sure – at least on the surface.

The crazy thing is, despite seeing through it and being repelled by it in others (we see it's all vanity, inch-deep), something in us *longs* for success on these terms. But much more interesting than skimming along the surface of 'success' is excavating deeper into some of the core motivating beliefs we humans have about ourselves, such as mistaken pride in thinking we each control our destiny, or paranoia that tells us there's an inherent scarcity of everything in the world. These are the swell that carry along the undercurrent of comparison – where we see the lives of others and long for a different reality for ourselves. And comparison – so often eliciting either pride or despondency – rarely ends well.

I've got what you want

A cursory glance through the wisdom of online articles on the matter tells us millennials typically understand that material wealth isn't the marker of success – there are enough old, sad, rich people to show that. Instead, success has now become synonymous with living a life that others want. Chase an experience. Go adventure. Wanderlust. #yolo. To succeed in life is to publicly consume as many unique experiences as you can during your short time on earth.

Social-media feeds are rammed full of early-to-mid-thirties enjoying a kind of spandex-clad transcendence. Success for today's generation would seem to look a lot less like the overweight suit-clad city trader selling their soul to the system, making shedloads of cash to buy a slice of suburban real estate with a Porsche in the drive, and more like the lithe and mindful global citizen doing 'life on my terms'. Think coastal living, yoga on a stand-up paddleboard in the morning, slaying the emails in your industrial co-working space, eating a superfood lunch, nailing a couple of zoom calls early evening before smashing some gua bao and margaritas with your peeps at the latest pop-up restaurant before taking an Uber home. #squadgoals

There's no escaping the fact that technology has shrunk the world and 'global capitalism has brought so many different ways of life closer to us than ever before. We can see vividly a greater number of people who we want to be.'[3] This can bring up hidden feelings we thought we'd buried long ago.

I often feel unfulfilled. Sometimes completely lost. For years I haven't been able to admit that. Until fairly recently I would find myself looking at others and thinking: 'Don't they ever struggle with life's big questions? Don't they ever want to give up? Surely I can't be the only one sinking under the weight of comparison?' Far from freeing me from my broken sense of self, the version of faith I was trying to live by was exacerbating the core wound

I recognised in myself. That wound was a sense of feeling a failure, unsuccessful. And like an unwelcome parasite, it fed on comparison to others.

About time

There's a recognisable concern underscoring much of the mainstream literature on success: *there is not enough time.* I don't mean being in a hurry in an immediate sense (though that's definitely a thing), rather a lifelong drawn-out feeling that, from cradle to grave, we apparently experience an acute fear that time is running out.

Read any random couple of articles on 'successful' people talking about how 'successful' they are, and a lot of what's conveyed is a profoundly angsty relationship with time: 'You only have one shot at life'; 'I don't want to waste my time on earth'; 'You can never get it back.'

It's as though we have an inherent recognition – and for some, dread – of the physical limits placed on us by virtue of being mortal and human. But what if unencumbered productivity, unceasing activity and unrelenting progress – however that is defined – are signs less of success than of self-centred insecurity? Could busyness really be the counterfeit of significance?

It's as if we have, left unchecked, an insatiable appetite for accomplishment. It's not hard to see where this comes from. Paul Kingsnorth comments that:

> Modern economies thrive by encouraging ever-increasing consumption of harmful junk, and our hyper-liberal culture encourages us to satiate any and all of our appetites in our

pursuit of happiness. If that pursuit turns out to make us unhappy instead – well, that's probably just because some limits remain un-busted.[4]

He goes on to suggest that this is a fundamentally spiritual problem, because 'a crisis of limits is a crisis of culture, and a crisis of culture is a crisis of spirit.'[5]

Mixing it up

The Bible tells us this life is just a brief moment in light of eternity – and so presumably, for the Jesus-follower, time isn't an issue. I wish this were true. Instead, we find that in many ways the culture of chasing the next, the more, the significant has snuck its way into the Church.

'Syncretism' probably isn't a word you use very often, but I think it might explain part of our problem with success. Syncretism means the mixing of different world views into faith, and at its worst it can dilute the message and subsequent power of the Church's witness in society.

Might we have adopted modern cultural norms into our faith, preaching feel-good messages of self-improvement, becoming more committed to tweetable soundbites than we are to the uncompromising words of Jesus? Do many of our lives just look like a slightly vanilla version of those who don't know the world-changing hope we claim to have living within us?

I'm not suggesting we return to some wholesale rejection of every-thing in the world, retreating to the desert and a purer pursuit of faith (though that has certainly worked at times in the past), but I am asking this: Would you say you're living in such a way that if

God didn't exist (and the life, death and resurrection of Jesus were untrue), your life would make no sense?

If you aren't, would you like to discover what you might be missing? (Disclaimer: often I feel I'm not and need reminding, so if you find yourself in this camp – you're welcome here.)

There is the most indescribably beautiful reality – more real than mere physical things – called the kingdom of God. It is all around us. Sometimes you just need to develop a new way of seeing to perceive it. I'm aware that to some of you this may sound a bit cryptic, and to others, what we've been through may make us cynical, but the kingdom of God really is a thing! In fact it was one of Jesus' favourite things to talk about – the rule and reign of God breaking in and manifesting on earth. It's what happens in us and through us as we lean into the power and participation of God in his creation. It's the little-by-little inbreaking of God's *shalom* – nothing broken, nothing missing – into the wounds of this world. It's the restoring of sullied images into the likeness of Jesus. It's the transcending-through-redeeming of what-once-caused-pain into something-that-now-brings-joy. It's the victory God promises and will eventually bring forth.

What is the effect of the kingdom of God on us? It is 'to align our loves and longings with his – to want what God wants, to desire what God desires, to hunger and thirst after God and crave a world where he is all in all'.[6] This different perspective for looking at the world recognises that *who* you are is primary to *what* you do, which in turn leads to a repentance that is less about being sorry for things you have done wrong and more about being sorry you are the kind of person who would do such things. In this way, the kingdom invites us into a life of deepening instinctive internal virtue rather than surface-level rule-following. It is often slow, sometimes painful, always liberating, and promises to make us thoroughly (un)successful.

It was when I recognised in me a deep desire to be more like Jesus and do things more like he did that I began a journey to unpick the sub-kingdom habits I'd picked up. I'd become, as José Humphreys puts it, 'fatigued by a gospel story too narrow for a complex and ever-changing world'.[7] This had developed into what looked like 'normal life' in a liberal Western society, and sometimes like a part of church that reflects – and is so often a product of – this society. Some of the joy and struggle of this journey of unlearning is what resulted in this (un)book.

Manenberg

I live and spend most of my life in a community that shouldn't exist. Manenberg is situated 20 km (12.5 miles) east of Cape Town's city centre and was built to house those categorised as 'non-white'. The homes of people of colour were demolished by the white supremacist government, and their inhabitants transported like livestock to newly built townships. Manenberg is one such community and stands as an obelisk of apartheid, a concrete reminder that structural racism is one of humanity's gravest injustices. And so unsurprisingly, being a white British guy, living in Manenberg can be complex because people who looked like me started this whole sad story. And despite many of my neighbours displaying a remarkable resilience in the face of grinding social issues, there is a lot of pain – pain that is both current and historic, personal and systemic. Even a good day in Manenberg can quickly descend into chaos.[8]

Along with some of our closest friends, my wife Sarah and I are part of leading a small, slowly growing church community in Manenberg called Tree of Life.[9] Currently we have two residential ministries – one for men seeking help leaving gangs and drugs behind, the other for addicted or abused women and their young children. Since I first moved to Manenberg in 2010, aged 24, the statistics on drug-related crime have got steadily worse year on year. It can often feel as though we're part of a well-meaning but ultimately futile attempt at doing something to bring lasting change to hurting people. So far we have only been moderately effective in seeing change in others, but the whole experience has been hugely effective in changing us.

There's nothing like being part of a relatively small group of people struggling to effect lasting change – in a community known for its violence, poverty and addiction, in a city characterised by spatial division, in the world's most unequal country – to feel as though you're not really succeeding at much, not really getting anywhere, haven't got much to show for your efforts. In this sense, the life we live is simultaneously the worst thing and the best thing for me: it triggers my comparison-driven feelings of failure with a fierce intensity; and so I have ample opportunity to work through them and see them transformed into something redemptive, something that points to the kingdom of God.

My life is pretty banal a lot of the time and, along with moments of triumph and celebration, is peppered with mini-defeats on a daily basis. Despite following the call of God to Manenberg, I can still feel decidedly powerless over my appetites; if you were to compare my time on social media versus time spent praying, it wouldn't begin to match up with what I'd tell you I value more. Sometimes, if I'm asked to speak somewhere, the person introducing me will say something along the lines of: 'This is Pete, and he and Sarah are the reeeeal deeeeal, they have given up everything to radically follow Jesus.' Then, in the same week, someone in Manenberg might say: 'What, Pete? The rich white guy who drives a nice car and lives in the quiet part of Manenberg?' I try to be present to both of these perspectives but defined by neither. You see, if I believe just one view as the truth, I'll feel like a failure: the 'reeeeal deeeeal' narrative makes me feel I'm failing in getting the church to see that following Jesus with our whole life is not radical at all, but if I internalise the 'rich white guy' narrative, I'll feel a failure for living in a poor community and having too much stuff. My point is, I do not write this book as someone who has got life 'sorted', living from revelation to revelation, but as someone who wants more of God's revelation – God's perspective – on who he says I am.

So now what?

Feeling you're a failure can be pretty exhausting. But, despite this, feeling compelled to present an outwardly successful, fully God-trusting public persona? That's even more so. I've tried both. Neither work. Maybe you can relate.

Thankfully there is a better way – but it's a narrow way. And so I'm starting to realise that, far from deconstructing faith, we need to learn how to transform it – taking what has been formed in us, seeking the Holy Spirit's help in *re*forming it, and watching the process of sanctification *trans*form it into something God can use to help us help others. It is this that enables our greatest wounds to become our most valuable contribution in the world.

Hence my writing this book.

I've discovered a different, creative, syncretism – one that has successfully brought me life and joy. I've begun to see the walls between religious, political or ideological categories as artificial and often a little silly. Though we've too often been taught to be suspicious of other parts of the Church, I've begun to embrace a faith that combines aspects of varying traditions. It's nothing particularly 'out there' or revolutionary, quite the opposite in fact – just a fairly conventionally minded embrace of the rich orthodoxies and traditions ensconced in the word 'Christianity'.

For example: the silent reflection of the Quakers, the prayerfulness of the Moravians, the hunger for miracles of the Charismatics, the unity of the Catholics, the simplicity of life of the Amish, the devotion to Scripture of the Reformed evangelicals, the peacemaking of the Mennonites, the revivalism of the Pentecostals, the liturgy of the Anglicans, the questioning of the deconstructionists, the commitment to the poor of the Liberation Theologians, the music of the Vineyard and Taizé movements, the strategy of the early Methodists, the stability of the Benedictines and the spiritual disciplines of the Ignatians.

God's nature is to create, and we partner with God when we offer creative ideas and share imaginative thoughts, not when we shut down or pull apart what currently exists. Condemning the Church is an easy pastime and there are plenty who spend a lot of time doing it, but things built on a negative tend not to generate hope. And so I have tried to ask not 'What is wrong?' (thereby trying to avoid shutting others down), rather more 'What is missing?' (thereby enabling the possibility for creative potential). I have tried to convey some of what I believe God aches for, so that we might understand better our role on earth and grasp the vision he has set before us.

It's easier for Christians to go along with how the world currently is than to imagine a different reality, and so we can be tempted to opt for convenience over faithfulness. But if we trade the heart of Jesus' kingdom with the values of the world, we will begin to forget that there is so much more of the kingdom of God for us to enjoy and for the world to encounter. I sincerely believe that if followers of Jesus catch his vision of true success, we will begin to see the Church come exponentially more alive – and so might just see the world around us begin to show more signs of the kingdom Jesus preached about.

You could define success as correctly directing your love and energy to what is primary and of most importance. While it's easy to become 'captivated by rival visions of flourishing' that much of today's culture tries to sell us, 'God has created us for himself and our hearts are designed to find their end in him.'[10] And yet despite professing faith in Jesus, many of us still spend our days 'craving rival gods, frenetically pursuing rival kingdoms'.[11] This is because there is no reorientating of our true selves and our longings without resistance from our shadow selves: 'It is crucial for us to recognize that our ultimate loves, longings, desires, and cravings are *learned*.'[12] I hope that the following chapters will assist you in (un)learning the disordered desires of the world, to make you more successful in living the life God has for you.

This is not 'self-help', it is 'Jesus, help'! And the success that Jesus modelled and taught can tend to look pretty unsuccessful in the world's eyes – it did get him killed, after all. It doesn't take a genius to see that the reality Jesus taught about is almost unrecognisable to, and increasingly ignored by, the world in which we currently live. Yet as you'll see, my loving motivation for what follows is this: I truly believe we were made to pursue lifestyles that exhibit both the supernatural power and the participatory suffering of Jesus – the most (un)successful person who ever lived.[13]

1

Success is ... Following God's calling over good ideas

How God wants to mess you up and waste your life

Deeper than our wanderlust and desire for adventure is our desire to find our way back home. Ultimately, we want the adventure only so we can savour it and tell it around the fireplace at home.
(Ronald Rolheiser[1])

I can only answer the question 'What am I to do?' if I can answer the prior question 'Of what story or stories do I find myself a part?'
(Alasdair MacIntyre[2])

I always told him, 'I trust you. I don't know where to go or what to do, but I expect you to lead me.' And he always did.
(Harriet Tubman[3])

Who am I? Where's my life going? What is my unique contribution to the world?

The experience of being a living, breathing thing is full of potential. Life can be a stunning adventure, a collage of evocative moments one on top of another, forming the layers of our very existence. It can consist of enthralling dreams being stitched together into a patchwork of profound accomplishments-in-the-making. But on the other hand, *boy* can it be difficult.

Weighty decisions, crushing setbacks, unexpected tragedies, moral dilemmas, humiliating betrayals, health scares, unrequited love, trapped wind. Added to that, we now live in a world that seems to be preoccupied with *doing* over *being*. Somehow the question 'What do you do?' has become the defining metric by which we are measured by others we have just met. As Jesus followers, we know we need another metric by which to measure 'what we do', but is the kingdom of God really the only perspective we in the Church are looking through when it comes to redefining what 'successfully' following our calling really means?

Where and who?

Before we can work out what our calling is, we have to look at the lens we are viewing this question through and the context in which we find ourselves. One of the greatest unforeseen gifts my wife and I are discovering in cultivating a multicultural church in a marginalised community is the effect that geography and community have on how we view a whole lot of things, from social issues and theological questions to church models and – you guessed it – calling and purpose. We are learning that 'our imaginations and longings are not impervious to our environments.'[4] This means that if our churches are full of 'people like us' we can be formed by a particularly narrow perspective, which can too often be internalised as 'Christian'. As Chris Heuertz reminds us: 'friendships that cross divisions of class, education, race, gender, ethnicity, age and ability are crucial for reconciliation and for the life of the church.'[5]

Before we wrestle with the topic of purpose, we must ask ourselves: 'How does where I live and who I'm in community with shape how I view the world?' Our opinions and views are not as objective as we think. I'm often reminded of a cartoon strip a friend sent me of a rhino wearing a beret, painting landscape watercolours. There are four frames of this friendly looking rhino, but whether he's in vineyards or mountains, beaches or cities, all his paintings have the same feature: smack bang in the middle, obscuring nearly everything else, is a huge grey horn. It's hard to see past this or view it as anything but a distraction. But for our artistic rhino, his horn is the first thing he sees every time he looks at something. We can critique it and say it shouldn't be there, but it's his reality one hundred per cent of the time. How we see the world and our place in it is less about what we are looking *at* and more about what we are looking *with* and where we are looking *from*.

The perspectives we are coming from, based on culture, upbringing, experience of trauma, faith or ethnic identity, may be so different from someone else's that it can be hard to find common ground. The problem is that we tend to view our cultural upbringing as normative, so we don't even see it; we can be unaware of the mono-racial, mono-theological, mono-cultural bubble we so often swim around in. We may have opinions on big societal issues – but do we have friendships that span them? We may think we know how God is guiding us – but do we have diverse voices speaking into our discernment?

Without a framing narrative of faith in Jesus we will turn to other things to find direction. Where mainstream culture seems to value flimsy platitudes ('If it feels right, do it'; 'With enough hard work you can achieve anything'; 'You deserve to be happy'), God's calling is rock solid. There's a profound distinction between being led by our convictions and driven by our favourite insta quote. While our feelings are real, they are a poor barometer to gauge what is good or true.

Calling is necessarily supernatural. It is the purpose of the God of the universe, communicated via some trans-cerebral means to each of his human children on our journey of giving our lives to the propagating of his love, beauty, truth and goodness throughout the world.

It's not that you *can't* make things happen in your own strength – many people spend their entire lives doing just that, some seemingly very successfully – but if God hasn't called you to that to which you're giving your life, you may be disobeying the one whose plans for you are inestimably better than your own. Disobedience to God can only end in heartache. This is absolutely not because he wants to punish you, nor because he's angry with you, but because you'll have given yourself to something less than his absolute best for you. And his best for you is what you were made for, is what makes your spirit leap and your soul come alive and causes not just your own flourishing but that of those around you. Whether you know him or not, whether you believe me or not, whatever your world view or cultural perspective, God brought you into being and has a calling on your life. He has planned in advance good works for you to do. Life – in this body, on this earth, at this time – is a journey of discovering what these good works are, learning to delight in them and then, well, doing them.

The thing is, it won't necessarily make logical sense.

It comes with a cost

A friend once shared a story at a large church meeting. That previous week he had felt prompted by God to give his car away to someone in need of one. As this would leave him car-less it would be an act of incredible generosity and obedience. Nevertheless, he did it. We all cheered. But the story wasn't over: a few days later, completely out of the blue, he was given an even better car by someone else. We cheered even louder. My friend was telling the story to show the goodness of God towards us as we faithfully obey him.

Immediately after the clapping died down, another friend stood up to reflect on this story: 'I just wish God hadn't given you another car!' The mood deflated. His point was that there's a real danger in telling testimonies where sacrificial obedience is rewarded with blessing, because the temptation for listeners then becomes to 'obediently' give things away to hold out for better things in return. This isn't generosity at all but manipulation wrapped up in materialism. My friend who shared his story of obedience and provision wasn't doing this, but it would have been easy to make a religious formula out of it. How many of us would give our car to someone if we knew that by doing so we would receive an upgrade? Probably most of us. How many would give a car away just because we had a feeling God was asking us to, without any expectation of anything in return? I imagine far fewer. But which of the two scenarios would we offer as the more 'successful' testimony?

There's a world of difference between only doing things that make logical sense or that come with obvious benefits, and walking the narrow road of obedience to God's voice. In seeking to attract people to faith, a theology of 'cheap grace' has sought to make the narrow path of the kingdom into a three-lane motorway. Cheap grace seeks to make the way of discipleship easy. It dangles earthly rewards in front of us as motivation. It promises reward without cost. It hides our light under a Christian-looking lampshade emblazoned with platitudes: 'God won't give me what I can't handle'; 'When he closes a door, he opens a window.'

If we live for cheap rewards we become short-sighted. If we make formulas out of God's generosity, we become entitled. If we cry 'Hosanna!' convinced that Jesus will give us what we want on our terms, we may well find ourselves shouting 'Crucify!' a week later because our needs haven't been met the way we wanted. It seems such an obvious point to make but let me say it anyway: success should not be measured by the 'blessings' or applause we receive, but by the closeness of our walk of faith to the 'blesser'.

What is our motivation?

When we find ourselves more obsessed with the blessings than the blesser, it is highly likely we are being at least a little motivated by a sense of *Geltungsbedürfnis*.

What – you don't know what *Geltungsbedürfnis* means? It's a brilliant German word meaning: 'the need to be recognised as valuable and worthwhile in the eyes of others'. Being praised for doing something others admire feels good. That feel-good factor can be much more of a motivator than we might admit: the praise of others can give us a strong sense of validation, and we can kid ourselves we really do have the answers to other people's issues. We can start to lose God in the very thing we long to do successfully for him.

The physician and public intellectual Hans Rosling reflected: 'Almost every activist I have ever met, whether deliberately or, more likely, unknowingly, exaggerates the problem to which they have dedicated themselves.'[6] I suppose we do this to implicitly validate ourselves. If you can frame the issue or cause you've chosen as *the* defining one of a generation (whether that's ending human trafficking, raising environmental awareness or funding donkey sanctuaries), and if you can brand it well, then you're on to something. Often the vision makes sense. It's a good thing to do. It seems to gain traction and looks successful. It's a worthy endeavour, offering 'scalable innovation', 'win–wins' and 'replicable models'. It seems to create employment out of nothing, receives coveted awards, accesses high-profile funding and celebrity endorsement as it *brings solutions to today's most intractable issues*. Add in the slickest social media that creates a kind of peer-pressure noise that generates FOMO for those not actively involved in it and you can find yourself with an organisation or ministry that gains traction and looks successful. The problem is, if the founding motivation is one of *Geltungsbedürfnis* rather than doing what God has called us to do, it will never be enough.

In language reminiscent of the Twelve Steps of Alcoholics Anonymous, Henri Nouwen references the Prodigal Son's quest for fulfilment:

> As long as I keep looking for my true self in the world of conditional love, I will remain 'hooked' to the world – trying, failing and trying again. It is a world that fosters addictions because what it offers cannot satisfy the deepest cravings of [our] heart … leaving us to face an endless series of disillusionments while our sense of self remains unfulfilled.[7]

In stark contrast to this, the love God extends to us and the wholeness that comes from being obedient to him provide the true approval we all long for. But sometimes that calling looks a little less flashy than the slick social-media portrayal.

But how much does it cost?

In complete contrast to well-marketed *Geltungsbedürfnis* campaigns, your God-given calling need not have anything to do with your networks, degrees, talents or education. In fact following God's calling may cost you all of that. You see, God reserves the right to waste any of your worldly accolades and qualifications, however hard you worked for them and however proud of them you are. I wonder if he delights in this; whether there's an intrinsic beauty in his sovereign 'waste' of our worldly labels. Not that he's deliberately facetious or particularly against your long years of studying medicine (or whatever equivalent). But it might just be that he prefers to use the very thing you like to think qualifies you for success in life, as something to give back to him in surrender, in exchange for his best for you. Could it be he might derive as much – or more – pleasure from seeing you wrestling deep down in your bones and eventually offering your years of professional credentials in an expression of yielding to his leading, as he would from turning you into a doctor?

Please don't misunderstand me. Qualifications are good. Education is a huge privilege (and so easily taken for granted). It's just that God doesn't call the qualified, he qualifies the called. I first heard this phrase from a Congolese friend standing at the front of a wonky, faith-filled wooden structure in war-torn Goma, preaching to a congregation of uneducated widows who were praying up a storm. Very few of them would have had professional qualifications or even a high-school education. In the eyes of the world, they weren't qualified for much. But the kingdom of God is a completely different reality. These women, in interceding for towns and villages across the eastern region of the DRC, and in sharing story after story of God transforming their lives and the lives of those around them, had dedicated themselves to a cause and emphatically displayed the power of pursuing their God-given calling.

John Wimber, who modelled obedience to God despite huge opposition, said:

> The economy of God's kingdom is quite simple; every new step in the kingdom will cost us everything we have gained to date. Every time we cross a new threshold it costs us everything we now have. Every new step may cost us all the reputation and security we have accumulated up to that point. It costs us our life. A disciple is always ready to take the next step.[8]

His words are basically a modern rendering of the Apostle Paul's resolute conviction in Philippians 3, stating that anything he had ever gained in his past he considered rubbish compared to what he now had in Jesus, 'for whose sake I have lost all things' (v. 8). While we may want to imagine a certain wistfulness in Paul's tone, remembering the convenience of the old days when he benefited from the abuse of religious power without being called to account for his actions, his subsequent words show no sense of regret at losing what he once had: 'But one thing I do: forgetting what is behind and straining towards what is ahead, I press on towards the goal to win the prize for which God has called me heavenwards in Christ Jesus' (vv. 13–14). Although Paul did at times leverage his Pharisaic past to curry favour with those he was telling about Jesus, the majority of his ministry flew in the face of his past training, accolades and reputation.

It doesn't take a particularly in-depth study of the Bible to find evidence of the seemingly illogical and sometimes completely baffling call of God on an individual, group or nation. Whether it's Abraham following the call of God to an unknown country, the Israelites walking through the Red Sea en route to the promised land, Gideon reducing his army by 99% from 32,000 to 300 to defeat the Midianites, or simply the peculiar combination of personalities and backgrounds from which Jesus chose his disciples – none would have been an easy job for the marketers. Among his disciples Jesus chose uneducated fishermen, a highly educated tax collector working for the Roman Empire (who we might call 'far right' today) and a zealot intent on overthrowing the empire (basically a revolutionary or anarchist – who we might call 'far left' today). He also chose Judas, who was a manipulator and thief. Hardly the most strategic or logical choices!

And I wonder if this is one of the hallmarks of recognising the calling of God on your life, as opposed to simply being driven by the excitement of a reasonable proposition or an exciting idea: that there is an innate cost to God's call.

Only one guarantee

The first chapter of the book of Jeremiah is an interesting one to reflect on as we consider the cost of following our calling, and how God makes that calling known to us. In verse 5 we read the word of the Lord to Jeremiah: 'Before I formed you in the womb I knew you, before you were born I set you apart; I appointed you as a prophet to the nations.' That's the kind of prophetic word many of us would love – affirmation that we've been set apart by God to travel to cities and nations and give them dramatic words of destiny (probably receiving multiple airline upgrades, such is the favour of God on us).

However, Jeremiah is not into it: 'Sovereign LORD, … I do not know how to speak; I am too young' (v. 6). His initial response is not: 'Right, let me set up a financial givers newsletter and launch a ministry website and get #setapart trending.' He's petrified by what God has told him, and there's not a hint of *Geltungsbedürfnis* narcissism. Instead there's a reverent fear. He recognises his weakness and protests against his commissioning.

But pivotally, he keeps listening.

And as he continues to focus on the voice of God, he gets a slap and a hug all at once. God essentially says: 'Grow up Jeremiah; you're about to learn that obedience to me is the only thing of value. I really don't care how insecure you are. Stop looking at what people will say or do. Just remember I'm right there with you.'

At this point Jeremiah's prayer-time-turned-life-changing-commissioning ramps up a level. God gives him visions and starts speaking to him through symbols that confirm the prophetic word. Jeremiah sees a picture in his mind's eye of an almond tree. Bit random? Well actually no. The Hebrew word meaning 'almond' is *shakeid*, which comes from the root *shakad*, meaning 'watchful'. God is saying he's going to hold Jeremiah to account to fulfil his prophetic purpose: 'I am watching to see that my word is fulfilled' (v. 12). Next, Jeremiah sees a vision of a boiling pot, tilting away from the north. This is just everyday imagery with no obvious connection to what has gone before, but again he hears what the meaning is behind it. God explains: 'From the north disaster will be poured out on all who live in the land' (v. 14).

So God's eyes are on Jeremiah, watching to see that he delivers a prophetic word to his people, who have turned from true worship to 'burning incense to other gods' (v. 16). Jeremiah's first commission is to speak out against the idolatry of Jerusalem and warn them that foreign kings with invasion on their minds are about to attack. And no, the people he's speaking to will not receive this well – he is to 'stand against the whole land' and 'They will fight against you' (vv. 18, 19). Pretty punchy stuff that few would relish and most would probably want to avoid or be done with pretty swiftly.

Jeremiah wasn't just obedient to God, he was obedient for the long haul. We go on to read that his prophetic ministry spanned roughly four decades. He didn't move on when things became less exciting, when he heard of a new move of God somewhere else or when he was misunderstood, didn't receive enough affirmation or see visible fruit. Nor did he shrink back or dilute his message. Once, after he'd been falsely thrown in jail, the king sent for him to ask if God was speaking. Without flinching, Jeremiah tells him straight up: 'Yes, … you will be delivered into the hands of the king of Babylon' (37:17). I don't know about you, but if I was stuck in jail and I got an audience with the one person who could set me free, I'd basically tell him whatever he wanted to hear. But Jeremiah doesn't flatter for his own sake – a hallmark of his life was faithfulness to calling God's people to repent of their idolatry and live lives of heart-motivated social justice and ethical reform. He did this over and over again, even likening the house of Israel's idolatry to the sex life of a lusty she-camel that couldn't be restrained in mating season (how about that for a niche prophecy).

His wasn't a ministry of baseless, surface-level ear tickling. There were no casual promises of prosperity and comfort or – a cliché in certain charismatic circles today – that they were 'on the cusp of breakthrough'. Instead, he called out those declaring peace in the nation when actually it was completely divided against itself: '"Peace, peace," they say, when there is no peace' (6:14). I'll leave you to make the connections with present-day realities. When false prophets were doling out feel-good prophecies, Jeremiah stood his ground and called God's people to commit to a long life in exile.

> Build houses and settle down; plant gardens and eat what they produce. Marry and have sons and daughters … Increase in number there; do not decrease. Also, seek the peace and prosperity of the city to which I have carried you into exile. Pray to the LORD for it, because if it prospers, you too will prosper. (29:5–7)

We often forget that these words were written to a people who had been forced into exile, who were asking deep theological questions about the goodness of God while struggling to deal with their anger and violent fantasies at the complete *lack* of breakthrough in their prayer life. (See, for example, Psalm 137, which was written during this time of exile and includes, among other things, promises of revenge and violent imagery of killing Babylonian children by smashing them against rocks. Some undealt-with anger there.)

Jeremiah didn't give them false hope along the lines that they should pray harder and make some positive declarations. He gave them guidelines for how to flourish in a place they'd never even wanted to be. This involved fuelling their prophetic imagination for what a life of shalom could look like at the apex of despair. Sounds epic? Well, really it's very ordinary.

It involved making home; toiling the earth, cultivating beauty and producing food; celebrating love and marriage, bringing up the next generation of family to know the ways of God. And – pivotally – it consisted in not losing heart in the face of the many unanswered questions and feelings of disorientation and abandonment, but humbly praying for the prosperity of the administration for which they did not vote but under which they now existed.

Throughout all of this incredibly costly and potentially quite anxiety-inducing call on Jeremiah's life, God makes two main guarantees. First, that Jeremiah would definitely be strongly and maybe violently opposed. And second, that God will be with him. This is not the promise of worldly success and human acclaim. This is a promise that says it will lead you, whatever the cost, into an even deeper sense of God's presence and that he will affirm over you once again: 'I am with you and will rescue you' (1:19). What if that's the only #setapart life that truly matters? If you only had those two guarantees, would you obey?

On whose timescale?

Whatever is going on around you, nothing you do for the Lord is ever in vain (1 Corinthians 15:58). But if you're in it for visible breakthroughs on *your* timescale, you'll probably end up giving up. As Jackie Pullinger so brilliantly points out: 'The problem is, we are expecting to reap the harvest we have sown – where most of the time we reap a harvest someone else has sown.'[9] What if the harvest you reap were to have nothing to do with what *you* sowed but is the direct result of the obedience of someone you will never know this side of heaven? Who knows if they saw any visible harvest to their labour. Who knows if they secretly battled with depression or discouragement for not seeing even a fraction of what you are seeing God do.

Have you ever scrolled through social media at the testimonies of others and become bitter that they've seen *results* already and you haven't? It's a peculiar kind of entitlement to expect the entirety of God's promises to be fulfilled in one's own life – talk about putting yourself at the centre of things. It's always right to pray for the power of the Holy Spirit to transform people, communities and nations, but we should be able to hold this in tension with the fact that: 'Showing everyone visible fruit does not make you successful. What makes you successful is doing the will of God.'[10] If instead of frantically pushing for success the way and when we want it we can come to a place of saying 'I need never see anything happen because I know I'm doing what I've been asked to do', then we're free from the scourge of success on any other terms but God's. And if God wills something, there is nothing we can do to stop it.

Rating Jesus

I wonder whether one of the main issues with the question 'What do you do?' is the subtle question lying underneath it: 'Does what you do position me above or below you?' If we're really honest, our old friend comparison is already at play before we ask this fateful question. The truth is, we've become so used to rating others that it's become second nature. You've just got out and closed the door of your Uber and your phone beeps asking you to rate your driver. Or minutes after you check out of your Airbnb your email pings and it's a request for a rating and review of your host. Whatever apps you use, wherever you are in the world, we have become fixated with attributing a numerical value to others' worth. All of these ratings cumulate into data, and data can too often signify how 'successful' we are in our culture today.

Naturally there are many professions that rely on quantifying things to measure success. Disaster relief workers counting the number of people fed or housed; fund managers calculating financial return on clients' investments; football managers analysing pass completion rates of two rival players; teachers marking pupils' exams. I'm not debating that numbers are important in many professions. I just wonder if the numbers don't always tell us much about levels of human flourishing or lives lived well. For example, how might it change the way you view success when many disaster survivors are fed and housed but turning to addictions because of suffering with post-traumatic stress disorder? Would you agree that success looks like high numbers when the hedge fund makes investments in companies polluting the planet in pursuit of short-term financial profit? Is it a successful coaching decision to buy the player with the higher pass completion rate but end up relegated anyway due to their negative effect on morale in the changing room? How proud a parent would you be witnessing your child's success in exams if to get there they sacrificed their emotional well-being?

There's something inside us that points to what lies deeper than data. I once asked online friends for their definition of success, and though I got answers ranging from the God-centred ('fulfilling God's will', 'well done, good and faithful servant') to the me-centred ('happiness', 'being the best you', 'three sane and loving children'), the majority pointed to a state of *being* rather than the result of *doing*. The quantifiable stats our world loves can't quite capture that. I mean, what would the data make of Jesus?

Jesus chose just twelve people to disciple. They let him down in Gethsemane, one set him up to be crucified, another denied even knowing him and they abandoned him right when he needed them. If judged on the success of his death on a cross, how did he do? Multitudes rejected him and today billions continue to turn down his offer of forgiveness and eternal life. One star? But if we look at Jesus through the only metric that matters – obedience to God – the facts tell a different story. He dealt with his fear and the anticipation of pain and rejection and allowed the authorities to crucify him unjustly. He yielded entirely to the Father's will. The resulting response from humanity is in one sense irrelevant. Whether everyone received this forgiveness, or no one did, Jesus paid the highest price to bring forth the greatest potential for new life. Then he rose from the dead, left the disciples with the Holy Spirit, and Pentecost comes. His followers preach fearlessly, heal the sick, cultivate subversive community, pioneer the redistribution of wealth and racial reconciliation, pray till walls shake and carry a movement that changed the world. Five stars?

Data can't capture everything but it *can* be used to tell a story – we just need to make sure we're concentrating on the right story. I wonder if some of the problem we have in holding obedience to God's calling in higher esteem than success in the world's eyes is that we forget that followers of Jesus aren't simply to live for the moment but are a *storied* people. Success nowadays is seen as starting something new or being 'self-made', and often focuses on the here and now. But what if that's a myth peddled by the un-storied individualism that prevails in the mainstream West? What if, biblically speaking, success is about joining in with the great cloud of witnesses who have gone before us in fulfilling God's plans to redeem the earth and make all things new? Obedience has been around for a long time or, as Eugene Peterson puts it, 'obedience has a history.'[11] He explains that in the same way we wouldn't trust the data and results of a poll that interviewed just one person, so we shouldn't trust our own solitary experience of God in isolation from the witness of history.

If we want to grow in the discipline of obedience to the voice of God then we need to cultivate a biblical memory by studying Scripture. As Peterson says: 'With a biblical memory we have two thousand years of experience from which to make the off-the-cuff responses that are required each day in the life of faith.' Not even the most crazed narcissist would have a problem conceding that one person's life is a miniscule speck in the grand narrative of the cosmos, which means: 'If we are going to live adequately and maturely as the people of God, we need more data to work from than our own experience can give us.'[12]

So let's look at some *storied data*. Hebrews 11 is a good place to start. To have faith is to have 'confidence in what we hope for' (v. 1). Hope is the fuel of obedience. We read that God told Abraham to leave home for a land he didn't know. Abraham 'obeyed and went, even though he did not know where he was going' (v. 8). A hero of the faith, he gave up the security and comfort of the known to follow the voice of God into the unknown. Right? So we are told by most preachers: 'Be like Abraham! He made his new home in a foreign land in obedience to what God had said and in faith that God's promises are true.'

But if we examine a little more of the data by reading the Genesis story, we also see that Abraham was part-time obedient man of faith, and part-time adulterous pimp. I've got to be honest: there are so many details in Abraham's story I don't understand – including the cultural customs of the time regarding marriage and relationships (about which commentators have differing views). But there do seem to be clear headlines to the story of his life, with obvious connotations for us now.

Abraham is presented as a man who is happy enough to trust God's overall plan for his life but finds it almost impossible to show this trust through obeying God in times of specific challenge. As time went by, some of God's promises seemed less and less likely – such as having a child when you're ninety-nine and your wife is ninety – so we shouldn't be too harsh on him. But despite his desire to honour God's promises, Abraham tended to make his own plans in moments of weakness – including sleeping with his concubine Hagar to conceive an heir of his own devices, and prostituting his wife Sarah twice, once to Pharaoh and again to Abimelech.[13]

His story can encourage and inspire us precisely because he is presented as an epitome of the human predicament – a mix of visionary and manipulator, faith-filled and yet controlling, courageous and careless, intuitive but also culturally conditioned. There's no black and white here and neither, probably, is there in your life. We're each of us a beguiling mix of contradictory virtues and vices – neither the summation of our best features nor purely the product of our worst. And if that's even a tiny part of the message of the story of Abraham then it comes as a great relief. The key is to ask: 'Who am I *becoming*?'

Rating yourself

My wife Sarah and I often encounter the question: 'What is your success rate?' It's a reasonable question but one that frustrates us enormously. We sometimes feel like asking back: 'We'll tell you our success rate if you first tell us what your success rate is in raising your children.' When associated with bringing up offspring, success seems an absurd metric to use. Something innate in us recognises that it's almost offensive to think about parenting in such a way. The fact is, we could answer the success-rate question in many different ways, from (forgive me) souls-saved-to-money-spent ratio, to the percentage, among the sixty or so young men who have come to live with us, who make a verbal and conscious commitment to follow Jesus. Worldly success in this scenario is meaningless because this 'success doesn't make sense of a self-giving love that is offered even to those who betray, deny, abandon and doubt us. But ... faithfulness in loving our friends – whether or not we see immediate results – does yield a harvest of fruit.'[14]

We need to reframe the question in light of the story of Jesus and those who have followed him through the ages: success in this instance is less about what you do and more about who you are becoming. Less about numerical results and more about your obedience to God. Only one metric matters. What if your unique contribution to the world is not primarily your talent, training or temperament? What if your unique contribution to the world – the most successful thing you could ever do – is first and foremost your yieldedness to God's voice?

Wrestling with these questions takes time. If you're following nice ideas devoid of the ultimate end to which God has orientated your heart, don't be surprised if you feel restless most of the time. Remember what St Augustine said of God: 'you have made us for yourself and our heart is restless until it rests in you.'[15] Your heart is not some sentimentalised notion, nor some quantifiable type, but the centrality 'of your most fundamental longings – a visceral, subconscious *orientation* to the world'.[16] In seeking to discover your orientation to the world, don't be surprised if you find you're fidgeting for God's best: 'To be human, we could say, is to desire the kingdom ... and long for a social vision of what we think society should look like.'[17] So embrace the fidgeting, lean into the restlessness you may be experiencing – scratch with a holy curiosity, for you were made to desire what God desires and before long you'll find that obedience to God's calling is so much better than simply good ideas.

Questions for reflection

1 What is your context? Who are you surrounded by? How might this be shaping the way you look at the topic of calling and purpose?
2 How do you define a 'successful' person, business or church? How might the things you're drawn to expose the desires or fragility of your heart when it comes to success?
3 Have you heard stories of people giving up something for God and getting something better? How does this encourage you? Do you think it can alter your motivation?
4 How does the idea of not seeing the fruits of your labour in your lifetime make you feel?
5 What has been stirring in your heart as you've read this chapter? Is there something you feel you need to repent or pray for? What might be the most obedient next step?

2

Success is ... Pursuing relationship over relevance

On friendship with God and people

We are divided between exploitation and nurture ... The standard of the exploiter is efficiency; the standard of the nurturer is care ... The exploiter thinks in terms of numbers, quantities, 'hard facts'; the nurturer in terms of character, condition, quality, kind.
(Wendell Berry[1])

Don't tell someone about Christ unless you're willing to give them your bed.
(Jackie Pullinger[2])

The spiritual journey is not a career or a success story. It is a series of humiliations of the false self that become more and more profound.
(Thomas Keating[3])

Do you struggle with the thought of going through life quietly unnoticed or being overlooked?

Me too.

The desire for obscurity doesn't come naturally to me.

What *does* come naturally is a desire for relevance – proving my usefulness to a world that demands I justify my existence through successful endeavours. Such 'success' is generally decided by the number of invites, online views and shares, by how many people are talking about us. But this tends to warp human interactions into opportunities to leverage things from others. And in that sense, relevance is the antithesis of healthy relationship.

Conversely, obscurity goes against this desire for prominence. Because obscurity is centred on relationship over relevance, it's all right with going quietly unnoticed. Christ-followers secure enough in their identity won't need public recognition. They'll happily get on with private acts of worship to God, good and loving things no one else need know about.

The professional business paradigm celebrates things that are high profit, scalable and generate more of something. If that's the model, then obscurity is one of the most subversive things we can go after in our quest for (un)success. There's an upward mobility many of us are expected to exhibit or aspire to that fails to bear in mind that of the thirty-three years of Jesus' life, thirty were spent investing in relationships, hidden in obscurity.

The American actor and writer Carrie Fisher shot to stardom playing Princess Leia in the original Star Wars films. Later in her life she came to realise that 'Celebrity is just obscurity biding its time.'[4] She recognised that however hard you might try to maintain relevancy and influence, at some point down the line culture will shift, wrinkles will appear, others will shoot to stardom, you won't get the jobs you used to, the public will move on and you'll probably be forgotten. This will happen to each of us.

That includes you.

Kick and scream all you want. Wail into the mirror. But if you quit thrashing around for a moment, calmly untwist your knickers and allow the gentle current of time to take you where it takes us all, you might begin to see the opportunity that obscurity affords.

In considering the powerfully transformative effect of obscurity I can think of few better examples than the journey of the late Catholic priest and author Henri Nouwen. After decades of relevance, moving among the intellectual elite as a lecturer at Yale and Harvard and writing a number of best-selling books, Nouwen chose to move to a community centred around relationship with the physically and mentally disabled in Ontario, Canada.

After twenty-five years as an academic and professional Christian, Nouwen confesses he was bad at prayer, disconnected from community and overly concerned with hot-topic issues:

> Everyone was saying that I was doing really well, but something inside was telling me that my success was putting my own soul in danger. I began to ask myself whether my lack of contemplative prayer, my loneliness, and my constantly changing involvement in what seemed most urgent were signs that the Spirit was gradually being suppressed.[5]

Please read that again: 'my success was putting my own soul in danger.'

Lack of prayer fuelled Nouwen's loneliness. Loneliness craves addressing urgent issues because it gives a sense of purpose.

But the Spirit was conspicuously absent.

This can be true for each of us individually but also corporately. Could a defective conception of success be putting the very soul of the Church in danger? By focusing on external relevance over relationship with each other, are we travelling on the same path as culture, viewing Church as franchise and people as consumers?

Oh no!

If there was something you and your family desperately needed, and you knew I had it and would give it to you if you just repeated some words I told you to, would you do it? Food handouts are an effective way to get hungry people to repeat the words of a prayer after you. But they are a questionable way of helping people follow Jesus.[6]

Or you find yourself walking along a noisy city street and you spot someone wearing a brightly coloured T-shirt and holding a clipboard making their way towards you. How does it make you feel? Targeting passers-by as statistics to sign up for your cause might be an effective way for a charity to buy more malaria nets, but it's a questionable strategy for the Church to use in introducing people to Jesus.

It's not that Christians shouldn't hand out food or ever engage in ministry on the streets, it's just that often how we do ministry that way points to a problem. Because:

> when communities have been saturated with missional activity, but the good news has not been embodied in a consistent presence of love and concern, folks know that they have been targets of one more program. And most of us resent being 'targets', no matter how well intentioned the effort might be.[7]

The problem is, we have disconnected three important things that need to go together: 'If mission isn't connected to discipleship within community, most of the efforts go nowhere.'[8]

Mission. Discipleship. Community.

These are not technical terms reserved for specialists, they are the foundations of our faith and should be central in our lives, whatever vocation we're called to. We've got to learn that in the same way reciting John 3:16 to a stranger in the supermarket isn't all there is to evangelism, a once-a-month meal after a church gathering isn't 'doing community', and joining a six-week programme doesn't constitute 'being discipled'. These, I would humbly suggest, are products of a church aiming for relevance over relationship in a culture that's a mile wide and an inch deep. If we want to be truly successful as church communities, we have to learn to put genuine friendship with God and people back at the heart of all we do.

The bottom line

Very often, though not necessarily deliberately, the Church can get a little too into counting people. The more people in our church, the more 'successful' we are and the more relevant to the world. This mindset tends to view mission in 'economic terms', adopting a 'sales approach' to a 'target audience', creating 'consumers of the product we're offering'.[9]

So now we've packaged Jesus into a consumer product.

Please read that again, slowly.

We need to consider not just the ends of mission (people reconciled to God) but also the means of mission (the way we represent God to the world), otherwise we undermine the people we're trying to reach as well as the message we're trying to convey.

In Cape Town we fairly regularly witness well-funded groups commuting into impoverished communities, handing out soap and food and posting about the 'miracle' of gangsters helping out – and when the groups leave, often the gangs end up fighting each other because they all want to sell the soap and food for profit. Then on a Sunday, buses are sent into the townships to take people to church miles away from their community, decimating the local church presence where it's needed most. I once spoke to a local pastor in Manenberg who vented his frustration with this approach: he was losing faithful congregation because his church couldn't offer them gift packs of food and toiletries. (That's not to say all large churches create problems in poorer communities – there are some wonderful examples I know personally of large churches with a healthy relationship to communities they serve.)

I do believe this finance-heavy, non-local approach is a sincere attempt to share Jesus. But it maintains the power dynamic between haves and have-nots and undermines any sense of building locally for the kingdom, sacrificing it on the noisy altar of smoke machines, generic worship experiences and handouts.

If we can see through 'evangelism as transaction' we'll be able to go beyond paradigms that present a need/solution mentality. There's an opportunity for mutual transformation that we miss if we think solely along the lines of 'You have all the need, I have all the answers.' In words often attributed to the Murri activist Lilla Watson: 'If you have come here to help me you are wasting your time, but if you have come because your liberation is bound up with mine then let us work together.'

We can only share in people's liberation if we know what is keeping them bound. We can only know what that is if we are in relationship. Relationships often bring us to the end of ourselves. The end of ourselves is where grace begins. And it's grace that transforms people.

Are you having a laugh?

I once took a young man from Manenberg to a majority white church in a well-off suburb of Cape Town. During the sermon, interspersed with quips about golf, the middle-aged white preacher made a joke about a largely industrial area of the city and how he would hate to live there. Everyone laughed. So far, so relevant. But my friend couldn't understand why this was so funny, because his uncle – the family member he most saw as a success – lived in that very area. For the preacher, a privileged older white man living in a comfortable suburb, this place was undesirable. For my friend, a materially poor young coloured[10] man living in a township, it epitomised success and achievement. I had taken him to church that evening to build him up and encourage him. But he left feeling humiliated.

We cannot talk about friendship without proximity. And we cannot talk about proximity without reference to where we are located. Such concerns are crucial if we are to reach those outside our church communities in ways that go deeper than a brief evangelistic encounter. The spatial history of Cape Town is evocative of the founding narrative of creation and fall: 'In Genesis, moving east is symbolic of moving away from God's design and favor.'[11] The townships of the Cape Flats, euphemistically called the 'Eastern Suburbs', seem to show this. Central Cape Town appears Edenic, but to the east, we are told, is crime and poverty. Going east reflects 'the world's desire for power, control and dominance'.[12] Jesus was crucified east of the temple. And today the majority of Cape Town is crucified by poverty and its effects, day after day, east of Eden.

So what does the journey westward look like – for Cape Town or your own setting? Abraham was first to move westward, post-Eden:

His journey westward was a yearning for the joy of Eden, a garden that would go against the grain of what society had deemed right and fitting, a garden of beauty and delight that would birth a new community, a new city.[13]

Most of what post-Christian society deems right and fitting is questionable at best. Would you consider going against the grain of conventional advice, cultivating beauty and delight in a quest to help form a new community in your city?

Henri Nouwen recognised that the success the world expected and even demanded of him – higher profile, increased production of content, wider reach – was making his soul sick, and he ponders whether the term 'burnout' is simply 'a convenient psychological translation for a spiritual death'.[14] It was in this season of questioning all he'd taken for granted that he began to take seriously the soul-harm of needing to maintain his relentless activity, and decided to move to a L'Arche community in Ontario.

He describes his move from the intellectual elite of Harvard University to the physically and intellectually challenged of L'Arche, 'from the best and the brightest, wanting to rule the world, to men and women who had few or no words and were considered, at best, marginal to the needs of our society'.[15] He went from leveraging high-profile relationships for the point of relevance and networks, to cultivating anonymous friendships of obscurity for the point of healing his wounded soul. The thing is, of course, that so often it's those of us who derive meaning and purpose from the influence our networks leverage who are most in need of soul-healing but least likely to go there. Or as Richard Rohr remarks: 'I cannot pretend to understand God, but this is what I see: People who have moved from seeming success to seeming success seldom understand success at all.'[16]

The desire to be relevant is the desire to be seen which, ironically, can only truly be found in relationship. I believe the journey 'westward' looks like friendship.

And friendship affects lifestyle.

The longing to be seen is embedded in us all. I was taught this by my daughter Simi. She isn't at all concerned about a lack of relevance, she just knows deep down she is significant and loved. Nobody taught her the game 'peekaboo' but at about twelve months she instinctively began to hide her face behind the arm of the sofa and then, in fits of giggles, would pop up in front of us. We caught on and began to do the same. This was too much for Simi, and she would often fall over from laughing so hard. There's not a lot to it, but at the core of the game is a feeling of delight in being looked for and being seen. Simi squealed in utter joy when her eyes connected with mine and I let out a high-pitched 'Peeeekaboooo!' She felt hilariously safe, seen and validated. We may want relevance because we want to be seen, but it is only in the most intimate of relationships that we truly can be.

If, as it's been said, we are likely to be most concerned for people we see first thing in the morning, then where we live and who we live with will shift our priorities. Reading the Bible first thing each morning with young men coming out of gangs and drugs reorientates my world as well as my interpretation of Scripture. I can never lose sight of the fact I'm from a middle-class British upbringing (and I'm thankful for some of the things it's given me), but I *can* choose proximity to people from entirely different circumstances to reorientate my presuppositions. And I hope my presence in the life of a young man from Manenberg whose upbringing led him into gangs and addiction can help him reorientate his own presuppositions. True friendship works both ways.

Nouwen understood that he needed to make a journey westward for the sake of his soul. You could say he spent the rest of his life journeying westward. He gives three keys for those of us seeking to follow Jesus (un)successfully, and each entails *movement*. These are:

1 from relevance to prayer
2 from popularity to ministry
3 from leading to being led.

Let's look at each in turn as we seek to better understand how the westward journey of friendship and obscurity over relevance can give us a different perspective on (un)success.

Movement 1: From relevance to prayer

The challenge of community living was a shock to the system for Nouwen, who had grown accustomed to an individualistic approach to ministry whereby he did his thing as a public speaker and academic and then went home to live his private life. But at L'Arche: 'Suddenly everyone wanted to know my whereabouts from hour to hour, and every movement I made was subject to accountability.'[17]

His first realisation about living with people with learning disabilities was that none of them were interested in any of the things he viewed as his strengths: 'Their liking or disliking me had absolutely nothing to do with any of the many useful things I had done until then.'[18] Friendship wasn't remotely based on the transactional potential one could offer the other in relation to reach, influence, power or prestige. Nor was it built on the premise of wanting to be seen with the right people or within the right networks. Those kinds of mindsets were completely absent.

The lesson Nouwen was learning is not particular to able-bodied and disabled, nor is it about the empowered and the disempowered. It's simply about the bridging of chasms of difference through the power of reciprocal relationship. Several years ago, three friends came to visit Sarah and me in Manenberg. We had a lovely week together, full of fun and deep conversations. But the day they left I'm embarrassed to say I sat on my bed and found myself crying involuntarily and completely out of the blue.

That week had been so affirming, so easy, so natural, so uncomplicated. I'd felt seen and heard and had been affirmed for my giftings. These visitors came from a similar background to my own, there hadn't been any awkward misunderstandings or cultural differences to navigate, and time had just flown by. The tears came on reflection of my profound frustration with the complexity and subtle nuances of building deep relationships in Manenberg; how painfully slowly things were progressing and how seemingly opposed cross-cultural friendships felt. And yet I blubbed myself to a realisation: that this was the very point.

Friendships with 'people like us' come easily. We tend to share similar humour, world views and life experiences. Friendships with those who in so many ways are completely different from us take so much more effort to initiate, grow and develop. Humour needs explaining, world views are often poles apart, and talking about life experiences – rather than creating a bond – tends just to highlight the sheer number of differences. Because such friendships are harder, they are rarer. Because they are rarer, their creative potential is so often missing from the world. And so authentic, long-term, relationships that go against the assumed grain of homogeneity and oppose the exclusionary logic of nationalism create bridges between all sorts of artificial barriers and disparate realities. What I regularly have to remind myself is that *that* is the point; *that* is the work.

As a white person living in a community of so-called 'Cape Coloured' people, and an Englishman living in a country and continent where my ancestors oppressed so many of all colours and cultures, I've come to see dialogue about race and power as pivotal to my own discipleship. In addition, for a local person in Manenberg to be friends with someone like me might not be viewed as a neutral thing due to past injustices 'my people' have committed against 'their people'. Addressing racial injustice is not a form of 'cultural Marxism'[19] but one of the most pressing invitations of the Spirit to the Church today. We need to wake up to such issues without falling for the catch-all progressivism of the age. It starts with friendship.

However, I'm embarrassed to admit there was a shadow side to my realisation: an internal voice was telling me I should specifically pursue friendships with gang leaders and drug merchants, well known and feared in the community, as that would extend my reach into Manenberg and raise our profile. (Oops, I mean Jesus' profile. Agh! Did my true agenda just come out?) That would surely be an efficient use of time and validate some need in me to seek power to extend reach. Some would say it's legitimate, strategic even. But there is a certain kudos attached to being seen with those with power in any sector of society, and that's no different in Manenberg.

I'm glad to say I've left that behind. But in the years that have passed since that awkward cry at the end of my bed, I've seen other outsiders come into Manenberg with the same intent of seeking proximity to power as proof of the effectiveness and success of their ministry. It rarely ends well. And so now if you tell me you're friends with certain gang leaders, or if you broadcast on social media that you've met with a well-known drug merchant, even/ especially if it's for the sake of 'Christian ministry', I'm immediately fairly sceptical.

I'm sure you can think of your own version of this in your field of influence. Nouwen recognised that our longing for relevance runs deep, and he implores: 'I am deeply convinced that the Christian leader of the future is called to be completely irrelevant and to stand in this world with nothing to offer but his or her own vulnerable self.'[20]

Nouwen saw the possibility for people to feel low self-esteem due to a perceived lack of impact – an increased busyness combined with a lack of visible change. The temptation to efficiency is to leave ministry and do something 'to make relevant contributions to a better world',[21] forgetting that persevering despite a seeming lack of 'results' may well be your most valuable contribution to a better world. In contrast, countering the world's logic of upward mobility:

> The leaders of the future will be those who dare to claim their irrelevance in the contemporary world as a divine vocation that allows them to enter into a deep solidarity with the anguish underlying all the glitter of success, and to bring the light of Jesus there.[22]

The angst that comes from dwelling on what others think of us and our achievements is created by a deep-set desire for relevance. Yet

Nouwen redirects our priorities back to relationship with the only one whose opinion matters. In simple terms, he states: 'The question is not: How many people take you seriously? How much are you going to accomplish? Can you show me some results? But: Are you in love with Jesus?'[23]

Movement 2: From popularity to ministry

Nouwen reflects that: 'Stardom and individual heroism, which are such obvious aspects of our competitive society, are not at all alien to the church.'[24] There's an element of this we hear in the reaction of people – outside of Manenberg – to the life Sarah and I and our Tree of Life community have chosen to live: 'It's such a noble thing you're doing'; 'What courage you have.' Such sentiments are meant well but they point to something deeply problematic.

Two prevailing false narratives imagined concerning life in Manenberg revolve around the ideals of heroism and romanticism. The hero narrative is disempowering because it conveys that obedience to the call of God is something exceptional when actually it's the most natural thing to do for someone who claims to love and follow Jesus. And all Christians are called to minister to the needy and broken – whether on the seventy-fifth floor of a shiny office block or on the dirt floor of a self-built shack. But there's absolutely nothing romantic about grinding poverty, the indignity of begging at traffic lights, having no home, being looked down on or ignored, getting sick from malnourishment and being able to think of little beyond daily survival. Both narratives are destructive because they're inherently paternalistic and remove the possibility for mutuality, where blessing flows both ways. We need to remember that: 'We are not the healers, we are not the reconcilers, we are not the givers of life. We are sinful, broken, vulnerable people who need as much care as anyone we care for.'[25]

So who will we learn from? Which successful business CEO or self-made mogul will we emulate? How slick and relevant and as like-the-world can we make our churches so that people new to faith won't feel uncomfortable in a new environment? Nouwen lays the smackdown:

> The world in which we live – a world of efficiency and control – has no models to offer those who want to be shepherds in the way Jesus was a shepherd … The leadership about which Jesus speaks is of a radically different kind from the leadership offered by the world.[26]

Jesus models leader-as-vulnerable-servant, and so his followers must exhibit a totally different way, 'not modelled on the power games of the world, but on the servant-leader, Jesus, who came to give his life for the salvation of many'.[27]

Bless you

There is something of a chain reaction that's set off when we become friends with Jesus. We receive the blessing of his faithful presence, his freedom from pains of the past, joy for life in the present and hope for what lies ahead. We also receive adoption into his family and experience his love for other people. It is the most natural thing in the world to desire for everyone to know this same blessing.

'Blessing' has become religious jargon, a spiritual-sounding cliché tending to refer to 'nice things God gives me for being good'. This is closer to greetings-card-platitudes than Christianity. Nor does 'blessing' simply mean – though it can include – God's favour and abundance. We know it must mean more because Jesus used it to describe very different states of being. In the Beatitudes, Jesus declares that the blessed are those who recognise their neediness, grief and pain, who desire more of God but who won't take up power to try and get it, who extend mercy to others, exhibit purity and pursue peace, and who will probably face criticism for all of the above.

With this in mind, I wonder if a reasonable definition of 'blessed' might be 'partakers of the divine nature' (2 Peter 1:4 RSV); to be someone not immune from the heartache of living in a broken world but, through sharing in the life of the trinity, somehow able to transcend the despair experienced by those who have not yet received this blessing. Trevor Hudson writes: 'Often the invisible ones are people whom our society writes off as no longer productive or useful … they yearn for the blessing that comes from being truly seen.'[28] In that sense, could it be that Hagar was as blessed as Abraham? Written off and no longer useful after giving birth to Ishmael, she encounters an angel, leading her to call God *El Roi*, 'the God who sees me'. In so doing she transcends the difficulties of life by partaking of the divine nature.

In societies across the world today it seems there is a pandemic of young people feeling overlooked and unappreciated, heard but not listened to, noticed but not seen.[29] God has so many different names in Scripture, but unless he is first *El Roi*, 'the God who sees me', he can't be any of the other names for me either. For *Jehovah Rapha* to heal me he has to see my sickness first. For *Jehovah Jireh* to provide for me he has to first see my need. The world generally projects characteristics on God by way of angry caricature. This is what enables people to reject faith – 'I couldn't possibly follow an angry, misogynistic god who condemns people to eternal torture.' Well no, nor could I. People desperately need to hear of the true nature of God that is *El Roi*.

So our message is: you may be lonely and feeling isolated but there is a God who sees all that, is with you in it and has provided you with hope for a way out through relationship with him – would you like to know him?

I see you

The greatest desire we can have for someone else is that they would know the blessing of God, to feel truly seen by their creator; that, like Hagar, they would awaken to the reality that God sees them, knows them and loves them inestimably. Of course, God has carried this love for each person since before their life on earth even began – it's just that not everyone wakes up to it in their life-time. This is an absolute tragedy and is the driving motivation for mission – we are privileged to introduce people to the love of God expressed in friendship with Jesus: 'To really see someone, whether they be a loved one or a complete stranger, is to give that person a special blessing.'[30]

The American author John Mark Comer made contemplative spirituality cool in his book *The Ruthless Elimination of Hurry*.[31] While it's not explicitly a book about mission, if our greatest missional objective is to introduce people to Jesus and we do that through showing them that God sees them, then our greatest missional strategy may well be to *slow down* – to eliminate hurry – so that we can first see the person in front of us. Hurry doesn't just harm me, it stops me seeing people beyond either their use to me or their external appearance. Only when we slow down can we see someone. And only when we see someone can we become their friend. And only when we have become *their* friend are we truly able to introduce them to *our* friend Jesus.

We saw this transpire during a particularly sad season of our life, when we were grieving the loss of a dear friend who had left gangs, drugs and Islam to follow Jesus but tragically died in a car crash. We were devastated and had closed Cru62 (the ministry we run to help gangsters and addicts find freedom in Jesus), to slow down and recuperate. One of the young men who had been living with us had stolen a considerable amount of stuff, including all we had left of our friend's possessions. And the final two had left and relapsed hard on to crystal meth. We were heartbroken, and it felt like everything we'd been working towards had both blown up and imploded at the same time. (We have subsequently got more used to this feeling, as the longer we do what we do the more we're able to see redemptive opportunity in the crises.) But what this did mean was that we had space in our home that was usually occupied …

One night Sarah had a dream about a mother and daughter needing a home. It seemed clear that God was reminding us to continue to be hospitable despite being in a difficult season, although we didn't know any mothers and daughters needing a home at that time. It was a couple of months later that an acquaintance turned up on our doorstep in his Toyota Quantum. As he got out and opened the sliding door, he just looked at us and said: 'You were the only people I could think of – can you help?' Sitting there was a woman and a young girl – a mother and daughter, huddled together in the back of the van. Without missing a beat, Sarah told the mother that we'd been waiting for them – God had spoken to her, and of course they could stay with us. The mother broke down in tears at the thought of God hearing her cries for help, going before her and preparing a safe home for her and her daughter by speaking to Sarah in a dream. We later learned, as we got to know them both, that she had an abusive husband, had been through unimaginable pain and trauma and was resigned to living on the streets. Knowing that she was not forgotten but *seen by God* changed everything for her. She wept and wept.

The next week our friend Dowayne was able to accompany her to the police station to lay a case against her abusive husband and help her obtain a restraining order. When we felt we were meant to reopen Cru62 she was able to move into another home with a caring family. I still sometimes see her when I'm walking around, and we always stop to chat and remind each other of the faithfulness of Jesus who sees us and blesses us.

In a world that disembodies human relationship by connecting relevance with number of views of online content, Jesus calls us back to the loving gaze of a Father who views delighted little girls, abused single mothers, celebrated academics and everyone in between – irrespective of how life has panned out – with the same eyes of compassion and affection.

Movement 3: From leading to being led

Before Henri Nouwen moved to L'Arche, when he was a professional academic, his confidence in his ability and leadership had grown and he felt increasingly able to control environments needing logic and order. But again this was fairly useless in his new environment at L'Arche, where 'all controls fell apart, and I came to realize that every hour, day, and month was full of surprises – often surprises I was least prepared for.'[32]

People lacking the intellectual abilities of Harvard students communicated not with ordered logic but with heartfelt emotion. As such, Nouwen found himself being led by his new friends, and learned lessons spanning the extremities of human emotion and experience, including 'joy and peace, love and care … about grief and violence, fear and indifference … what I could never have learned in any academy'.[33]

Now you don't need to have the title of 'leader' in your job description to concede that most of us have a bent towards wanting to lead. While you may not feel especially gifted in or passionate about being in charge of a team of people, presumably you would prefer to pursue your own vision, on your terms, rather than just follow someone else's. (Incidentally, this is often a reason people give for not wanting to put their faith in Jesus – discipleship is reductionistically viewed as 'following a set of rules', and we don't want anyone else telling us what to do.) We all want the perks of a freelance lifestyle where we need answer only to ourselves. Maybe we've got disillusioned with toeing the party line, working for a toxic boss in an uninspiring work environment, or perhaps we feel like we don't fit in and are getting nowhere in our career. In a heady haze of autonomy, we quit, set up our own thing, call ourselves an entrepreneur and finally feel like a proper adult. Or at least what we imagine a proper adult would feel like. But it doesn't take long before we come across the inconveniences on the other side of the coin: no steady income or paid sick days.

In his conclusion to the whole thing Nouwen reflects how moving to L'Arche showed him 'how much my own thinking about Christian leadership had been affected by the desire to be relevant, the desire for popularity, and the desire for power'.[34] He had now come to realise these three things are not strengths to develop but temptations to resist, and that leading like Jesus looks entirely different from what we tend to imagine. We think it's going to mean relevance, popularity and power, and he takes us 'to places we would rather not go. He asks us to move from a concern for relevance to a life of prayer, from worries about popularity to communal and mutual ministry, and from a leadership built on power to a leadership in which we critically discern where God is leading us and our people'.[35] The problem is that the old ways work to some extent – there's an efficiency to them. They get things done and feed our shadow selves at the same time, both of which feel good.

The writer of Proverbs gives us some great advice here:

> My son, do not forget my teaching, but keep my commands in your heart, for they will prolong your life many years and bring you peace and prosperity. Let love and faithfulness never leave you; bind them round your neck, write them on the tablet of your heart. Then you will win favour and a good name in the sight of God and man.
> (Proverbs 3:1–4)

Success equals love for others and faithfulness to God's calling. End of story.

Our problem, as we have seen, tends to be that we pursue favour and reputation as our *end* but forget about love and faithfulness as the *means* to it – we do literally the opposite of what Proverbs talks about. The earlier in life you can do the ego work the better. And then you never know, you may end up leading something big because God can trust you. But if you don't, you won't mind because you've become mature enough to be unmoved by visible success as a motivator. You've given yourself to love and faithfulness and the result is you're now so full of peace and prosperity that worldly accolades are irrelevant. You will be able to say, with Bonhoeffer: 'The figure of the Crucified invalidates all thought which takes success for its standard.'[36]

This and that

My friend Clare is not only one of the best preachers but also one of the most relational people I know, seemingly so free from the pursuit of success on the world's terms. At our Tree of Life gathering one Christmas, she spoke on the dialectic of the Christian life:

As I look back on this year in our family, I see so much pain, so much sin, so much brokenness. We have mourned death together, we've seen people relapse, friends choose death rather than life. We've seen doors close, systems that are supposed to protect the vulnerable fail. We've seen sickness, homes on fire, relationships break down ... it's been a hard year. But we've also seen marriages, births, children writing their names for the first time, young men and women choosing life bravely, day after day. We've seen family rise up to support one another, we've seen people get book contracts, get jobs, travel overseas for the first time. People became qualified, relationships restored, we've seen people get clean and stay clean, we've seen our family grow, we've seen miracles, healings of wrists and legs and hearts ... this has been a good year. We live in the middle of joy and pain, of celebration and suffering, of life and death.[37]

For those who prioritise relevance above all else, deep relationship with God and each other will seem slow and inefficient. Relevance doesn't have time for such tension – it simply looks to what is necessary to transmit a message. But might the things that are most good and beautiful also be the most unnecessary? The story of Waydin travelling overseas for the first time is worth telling because it is unnecessarily beautiful.

Waydin came to us after being thrown out of home and living in a car in a neighbour's yard. Up to then his life had consisted of running from the trauma of his past through smoking crystal meth and committing violent crime as part of a gang. Eighteen months in Cru62 had led him to faith in Jesus and changed him beyond recognition. To celebrate his graduation from Cru62 we took him to a 24-7 Prayer gathering in Vienna. He had never been overseas and was beyond excited to fly for the first time. When we got to the airport he was feeling nervous and asked me to accompany him to the check-in desk to help with any questions he didn't know how to answer. He handed his brand-new passport to the airline employee, she opened it, flicked through it to check for the visa and ended up at the photo page. Immediately her head shot up and she looked Waydin in the eyes.

'Waydin?!' she yelped.
'Faieka!' he replied, beaming.

Faieka was Waydin's next-door neighbour – they had been friends growing up together, and she'd watched him start taking drugs as his life unravelled into gangs and crime. Now here he was, years later, looking like a different man. Faieka was a Muslim, and she stared at him in disbelief as he shared his testimony. For the people behind us in the queue it was the slowest check-in they would have experienced, but that couldn't have been less important to Faieka in that moment. Of all the airlines we could have chosen, all the days we could have flown, all the employees who could have checked us in, God decided that it was time for Faieka to know that he saw her, knew her and was speaking to her. And he used a long-forgotten friendship to convey his love.

East of Eden

There is a great irony to living in Manenberg and travelling in an aeroplane. The townships of the Cape Flats, 'east of Eden', surround the international airport. This was conceived of and built by the apartheid government and means there's no shortage of local cheap labour serving the flux of travellers. Yet despite the aeroplanes coming and going with such noisy regularity and proximity (flying as they do right over township shacks), international travel remains a unattainable dream for the vast majority of those who live closest to the airport. This neatly sums up the disconnect of living in a globalised world where people can simultaneously benefit from and feel imprisoned by it, for 'Mobility, and control over mobility, both reflects and reinforces power.'[38] We could now add digital mobility as that which reflects and reinforces power.

The innate craving for bigger and wider is exacerbated by what some call innovation. Dissatisfied with the smallness of the work, there is a restlessness in the Church to conquer more territory, whether wider networks, increased funders, more ministries, better-selling books, more public recognition or higher-profile platforms. And the thing is, we often applaud that. We look on and say 'Wow, that shows God is really doing something amazing through you!' But now more than ever it seems to me there's a prophetic mandate: the Church needs to be 'committed to its context, to the local as the key to the global, to the concrete, and to the necessity of praxis'.[39] It may be this that keeps our souls from becoming sick. To be committed to the local over the global means recognising 'the opportunities and the limits of life in *this* body, *this* community, *this* set of relationships, *this* financial situation, *this* place where we have been called by God to serve'.[40] And that means committing to friendship with the people around us over trying to grow relevance with the masses.

Focusing on local engagement means we have to look at how to maintain healthy relationships. We have stumbled pretty far from the core of the gospel message as lived out by the early church, which:

> followed the Spirit ... and found deep wells of God's grace among the poor and excluded. Communities composed of oppressed slaves, marginalised foreigners, uneducated women, and all manner of improper and unacceptable people

found a place of hospitality around the table set by the early followers of the Way.[41]

But to navigate such a broad spectrum of perspectives successfully is not easy. If we want to cultivate friendships that reflect the kingdom and endure through thick and thin, we need to learn about betrayal and forgiveness. This is no easy journey.

One Christmas recently, Sarah and I went to visit my family in the UK. Spending time playing with our nieces, sitting in front of roaring fires, consuming an indecent number of mince pies, drinking murky room-temperature ale in crowded pubs with wonky walls and shiny worn stone floors – those were the sorts of thing I missed living in South Africa. Things had been running well in Manenberg. Cru62 was thriving and full and life felt good. We were even beginning to dream of expanding our space. However, a couple of days after returning home some distressing truths emerged – resulting in Cru62 having to close and a long, hard journey of restoration and re-establishing trust. It took us months to process and come to terms with what had happened and it hurt us both deeply. It felt as though what we'd spent years building had been completely ruined – by someone we loved dearly.

Betraying those we love

The experience of betrayal 'is part of the metanarrative of all great human stories ... [and is] one of the perplexing and peculiar gifts that comes from weaving our lives together with others'.[42] The big question it makes us ask is: 'How am I going to respond? Revenge or forgiveness?' Jesus demonstrates that true success starts with forgiveness. Rather than seeking revenge, we learn to entrust ourselves and others 'to him who judges justly' (1 Peter 2:23). If Jesus was betrayed, having loved so perfectly, we who love so imperfectly will also be betrayed. But here's a question: if betrayal isn't deliberate, is it really betrayal or does it just feel like it?

We betray ourselves before we betray anyone else and we do it all the time. When was the last time you acted, thought or spoke in a way that went against your deepest-held convictions and most cherished values? Perhaps it was the cutting words you used to humiliate someone in a group; the overly aggressive disciplining of your child; the financial investment you made in a company you knew to have questionable ethics. There's always a reason we can give for why we do it, and although we may rarely do it in the company of others, in the secrecy of being alone it may be fairly instinctive.

Relapse on to a substance can be a classic example of betrayal. If someone you love relapses despite all the help you have given them, you may *feel* betrayed. But bear in mind that in relapsing they betrayed themselves first. They chose to bypass their deepest desire in life (staying sober) in favour of their strongest desire in that moment (to use drugs). And the chances are that the thought process leading to relapse didn't consider *you* at all – isn't it interesting how often we put ourselves at the centre of other people's stories (but that's a whole other subject)? And so if you weren't even in the equation were you really betrayed? Mainly it's our inability to live up to the best version of ourselves that lets people down. It's often not an intentional act, just a result of momentary failure to resist our shadow self – and so: 'Many of the times when we fail our communities and those failures are experienced as betrayals, it's safe to say that we don't realize what we're doing.'[43]

Why is this? Well, we are all a culmination of our past experiences to some extent, whether positive and affirming or negative and destructive. Heuertz remarks:

Some of us have never been loved the way we needed to be and subconsciously carry our wounds into our relationships by not knowing how to love others well ... Though we attempt to love, the inadequacy of our ability to do so well is often experienced by others as a form of betrayal.[44]

When we first make a commitment to follow Jesus, we are changed. To use biblical language, we have been 'born again' (John 3:3) and have become a 'new creation' (2 Corinthians 5:17). But we still need to learn how to practise the way of Jesus day in, day out, and we will often get it wrong. If we had a particularly tumultuous life before meeting Jesus, then there might be a lot to unlearn and get free from. The idea of being able to recognise and name different feelings at work in us – let alone the *needs* behind such feelings – may be an entirely new one. And because each of us is at a different point on the journey, because we're all triggered by a unique set of memories and wounds and because the nature of blind spots is that we don't see them, this goes some way to explain how we hurt each other so much, despite our honest desire not to. But I'm not sure this is betrayal; it's just learning to love people better by loving them badly at first. Or it's discovering what hurts them and then trying to do it less. As such, 'most betrayals are simply immature expressions of love.'[45]

You can give years of your life to pursuing friendship with people not like yourself in an effort to grow mutuality and humility. You can go deep with one another. You can expose your latent loyalties to cultural prejudice. You can posture yourself to listen and learn rather than talk and teach. You can look for opportunities to give away power and to serve. You can confide in and confess your darkest secrets and together pray through deep wounds. You can do all this and more. And still you can end up betraying each other.

The Church needs to work out how to navigate betrayal – particularly if we are coming out of traumatic backgrounds or lifestyles of addiction and abuse, where hurts are so often transferred on to those closest. There's nothing more valuable or instructive than being betrayed by someone you love dearly – and into whom you've poured so much of yourself – for showing you just a fraction of the heartbreak and patience God must feel towards you each time you let him down. As in relationship with God, so in friendships with people – betrayal doesn't need to define or mark the end of the relationship.

If, as I have come to believe, there simply aren't quick fixes to decades of addiction and abuse, generational sin in reaction to pain, or the allure of deformed desires sold to us by the world, then friendships with those navigating such emotional complexity will rarely be straightforward. But that's no reason not to pursue such friendships in the first place – indeed, maybe that's the greatest motivator *for* pursuing them. Because as your pain hits my pain we learn to lament as we both fall to our knees in greater measure of surrender to the only one able to release us from our pain. Of course, there are times when someone receives a miraculous healing, physical or emotional. This is equally effective in bringing a co-humility in friendship as both parties witness the Holy Spirit doing what neither of them possibly could.

It's all about fruit

There's no escaping it – this is hard work. But have you ever met a Christlike person with an easy past? And I'm pretty sure we're called to both *bearing* fruit that lasts and *being* fruit that lasts. This means we need community around us to remind us how to hold on to faith and hope patiently, because: 'The opposite of patience isn't impatience; the opposite of patience is unbelief.'[46]

So how do we grow in patience, keeping unbelief at bay as we grapple with such deep complexities? Or 'when we develop friendships with people who are quite different from ourselves in terms of power, resources or life opportunities, what practices will help us maintain integrity and faithfulness?'[47]

The answer is friendship.

Friendship with God.

Recognising our belovedness.

As we generate practices that enable us to focus on this truth, we draw nearer to Jesus. And the closer we are to him, the more we desire to love others. So we initiate ways to grow friendship with people. And as we experience both joy and pain through human friendship, we are brought back to drawing near to Jesus. And the cycle continues.

1 I draw near to Jesus in friendship.
2 Being truly seen by Jesus helps me see others.
3 Seeing others leads to friendship with them.
4 Human friendships bring both liberation and joy, and pain and complexity.
5 These emotions cause me to draw back to Jesus in dependency and friendship.

If we can live in this cycle we needn't burn out: 'Love is not a scarce commodity ... friendship with the source of love guarantees that we will have sufficient supply.'[48] 'We love because he first loved us' (1 John 4:19). What do Henri Nouwen, Hagar, my daughter Simi, an abused single mother in Manenberg and Waydin's friend Faieka all have in common? Each of them has experienced being truly seen and known by God in the deepest parts of their soul. And from this place of being 'seen', each is on a journey of being (un)successfully transformed.

Questions for reflection

1 What comes more naturally to you – a desire for obscurity or visibility? What do you think might be the motives behind your answer?

2 Are there relationships in your life that are one-sided? How can you change your interactions with these people to make room for reciprocal friendship?

3 When have you felt truly seen by God or another person? How did it feel? How could you see someone else?

4 Which of Henri Nouwen's three movements appeals most to you? Which do you feel most resistant to?

5 Have you ever experienced betrayal? Has this chapter changed the way you look at it? When have you betrayed yourself? How do you feel about the idea of betraying God?

6 What has been stirring in your heart as you have read this chapter?

3

Success is ... Growing in depth over volume

Why influence looks different from what we've been told

If there is a problem somewhere this is what happens. Three people will try to do something concrete to settle the issue. Ten people will give a lecture analyzing what the three are doing. One hundred people will commend or condemn the ten for their lecture. One thousand people will argue about the problem. And one person – only one – will involve themselves so deeply in the true solution that they are too busy to listen to any of it.
(Elias Chacour[1])

The church is like a swimming pool. Most of the noise comes from the shallow end.
(John Shelby Spong[2])

We live in a noisy place, inside and out, and the noise we hear pours into the noise we make.
(Francis Spufford[3])

Influence is a very current thing to talk about. People are obsessed with influencing others. If you're reading this, it's most likely this book got published. Yay! But let's be honest – getting published is becoming less and less about writing a publishable book. It relies on having and growing a following, committing to staying current by blogging, looking for opportunities for stage time, leveraging networks, trying to raise profile – the list goes on.[4] The definition of a successful book is that people read it and are transformed by it, and to have people read it you need to influence them to buy it.

And that's *Christian* publishing.

And this is a book about being *unsuccessful.*

Oh the irony.

It's really hard to think of ways to promote this book that don't undermine its very message. I mean, this chapter is a critique of self-promotion and the noise all around us. So I shouldn't add to that, right? And yet to be frank, I think it's a pretty good book and would love for lots of your friends to read it. So can we just lean into the tension for a moment?

Fine. Thanks – let's move on – where were we?

Yes: influence.

Social media is full of it – even as we are trying to influence our followers with our views and lifestyle advice, we are unwittingly being influenced by big-tech companies and their agendas to keep us online for as long as possible.

Politics is full of it – if a politician can get people onside with the right views on the big issues, if they can play the game of optics and opportunistic soundbites, they can influence you to vote for them whether or not they have the character to lead.

We live in a world where being an 'Influencer' is a job. It basically involves filming yourself (a lot), trying to get people to buy certain products or endorse opinions you're sharing, or simply sharing with us your highly curated life to which we're meant to aspire.

Influencer influenza

On some level I wonder if engrained into contemporary Western culture is a belief that bigger is genuinely better, and whether this fixation with size and numbers comes from our acceptance of capitalism as a kind of default setting for humanity. I'm aware that blaming capitalism for all the world's woes is 'so in' right now, and that few of its critics offer anything better in return. All the same, we've become used to competing with others; economically we celebrate outgrowing the opposition; and strategically we're trained to produce the most, the quickest, the cheapest, the best. It's certainly something I've had to unearth and unlearn in myself.

I first noticed it one afternoon as I was having tea with two old ladies a couple of hours' drive from Cape Town. I'd been put in touch with them by a mutual friend who evidently thought I could do with wrestling with some hard truths. It was clear they'd been round the block ministry-wise, and they took turns recounting stories of the faithfulness of God over the years. I began telling them a bit about what was going on in Manenberg and my desire for our church to gain influence, reach more people and change many more lives, but that this would require more support and more volunteers. As I carried on, I noticed one of the old ladies' sparkly blue eyes begin to narrow and she screwed up her already wrinkled face. She interrupted me, shaking her head and putting up her hand like a police officer signalling traffic to stop. 'No, no, no!', she said:

Be careful! More isn't always a sign of growth. You can grow in influence, have lots more people, more money, more buildings, you name it – but if you haven't grown in the presence of Jesus among you and in his love for the poor, then what you're talking about isn't healthy growth at all. It's just swelling. And swelling is what happens when something is infected or broken.

A few years after this conversation I received a phone call from a YouTube influencer (the one time it's happened, in case you're wondering). He was a friend of a friend and was calling to ask if he could bring a group of fellow influencers to Manenberg, to see some of Tree of Life's ministries in the community and maybe play with some of the kids. (Can you imagine a London-based crèche or pre-school allowing complete strangers with no police clearance forms to come and play with the kids? We would be outraged. But I digress.)

If I'm honest, there was something quite attractive about the suggestion. Who knew – maybe Tree of Life would receive a flurry of online hits through the content and tagging of this group of visitors. My mind began to wander: maybe this would grow our funder base – we're struggling financially, so that would mean we could pay staff. Also, couldn't this be an opportunity to leverage any increased profile for the good of those who need help?

And before I knew it, I'd been infected with viral aspirations. I'd forgotten the advice of the old lady because the glittery allure of trickle-down economics had me transfixed. The problem was, we would be at risk of completely undermining the depth and integrity of our presence in Manenberg by broadcasting noisy poverty porn to the world via selfie sticks. It had taken – and continues to take – years to grow trust within a community used to outsiders coming in, taking what they want and then leaving again. I knew this. I'd had many conversations and heard the frustration of friends in Manenberg lamenting being objectified or their plight being used for others' gain. And yet it took me about two and a half minutes of daydreaming to fall completely for the temptation to put noise over depth.

I came to my senses and said 'no' to the request.

There's something about the allure of influence that really appeals to the ego – that narcissistic shadow self – that each of us possesses. Sadly the Church can be full of it. We all succumb to hidden temptation sometimes. We all struggle internally to measure up to the life we present externally. This is part of the very nature of being human.

Easy to do, hard to admit.

The issue with influencer culture is that it intentionally glosses over such realities and presents us with a shiny-but-broken conception of reality. If church leaders, and Christians seeking influencer status, try to mimic this, could it be any surprise if churchgoers choose noise over depth in their struggle with desire for influence?

Doing what he was promising

As N. T. Wright helpfully reminds us:

> The whole point of what Jesus was up to was that he was doing, close up, in the present, what he was promising long-term, in the future. And what he was promising in that future and doing in that present, was not about saving souls for a disembodied eternity, but rescuing people from the corruption and

dccay of the way the world presently is so that they could enjoy, already in the present, that renewal of creation which is God's ultimate purpose – and so that they could thus become colleagues and partners in that larger project itself.[5]

This quote captures the essence of Jesus' life and ministry and describes something of the inner desire of the current generation. Look particularly at how Wright says Jesus was doing in the present what he was promising in the future.

That matters.

Jesus was the antithesis of a selfie-stick-wielding influencer competing for attention. But all too often the Church comes across as such. We have something we're desperate to flog to the masses but the masses aren't convinced because we're not doing in the present what we're promising them in the future. Or as James Baldwin famously put it in another context: "'I can't believe what you say," the song goes, "because I see what you do."'[6]

We won't know true influence unless we are able to display true integrity.

Jesus has called us to bear fruit that lasts. It seems we are still trying to work out what that looks like and how best to achieve it. But the fact is there's a world of difference between the quiet, almost unnoticed nature of the mustard-seed or yeast analogies Jesus used to describe his followers' influence in the world, and the loud, self-congratulatory nature of an influencer's public presence in society. We get to choose which we allow to influence us.

Tiny mustard seeds quietly growing unnoticed but eventually becoming a tree able to offer shade and shelter under its branches;

brown dirt-like substance mixed in with flour and water that you would never even notice was there – until it causes everything around it to rise and grow. Unassuming, unshowy, easily missable but quietly transformative – that's how Jesus chose to describe the kingdom of God. In complete contrast, C. S. Lewis's Screwtape tells his demonic minions, 'We will make the whole universe a noise in the end.'[7]

No place for that

The author Kyle Chayka coined the term 'AirSpace' to refer to 'the realm of coffee shops, bars, startup offices, and co-live / work spaces that share the same hallmarks everywhere you go'. He remarks that: 'The homogeneity of these spaces means that traveling between them is frictionless ... Changing places can be as painless as reloading a website. You might not even realize you're not where you started.'[8]

Is it any coincidence that the literal meaning of the word 'utopia' is 'no place'?

With the rise of globalism in the 1980s, as technology advanced and communication and travel became easier, external links *between* cities were seen to be as crucial as internal dynamics *within* cities. So began the process of transcending cultural, national and geographical barriers in the name of capitalist endeavours.

Today we are witnessing churches and Christian organisations moving towards becoming 'international' church and 'global' organisation in a quest for greater influence. I think it's problematic for at least two reasons: it creates spiritual consumers and it exacerbates inequality. If our faith is as much about collective reconciliation with our fellow humans as it is about personal reconciliation with God, then trans-local digital content at best can only produce 50% of the goods. No amount of leadership podcasts or Instagram Live can substitute for the depth of real, embodied, face-to-face discipleship.

As the Church grows in catering for the digitally empowered young professional it will risk forgetting about those who can't afford a smartphone or device or the mobile data costs (relatively much higher as a percentage of income in the Global South). Contrast this with something I read recently on the website of a well-known Christian leader. He declared confidently: '... everyone you want to reach is online. If you miss the Internet, you miss them and all the opportunity that comes with it.'[9] I wonder how he interprets Isaiah's words that the Spirit of the Lord is upon us to preach the gospel to the poor. I wonder what he makes of the stats that tell us the fastest growing demographic in the world is the urban poor – many of whom won't have access to gigabytes of data.

It's a curious ecclesiology that suggests anyone without an iPad is doomed.

In stark contrast to this supposed digital utopia, the Scriptures convey physical place as being inherently relational, and this is conducive to divine encounter. There is a dynamic interrelationship between place and story, people and God. Lose place, lose story, lose encounter. As John Inge writes: 'If places are the geography of our imagination, it is ... true to say that how we are affected by them will be a function not only of the place, but of the people we find in it.'[10] The linking of place and people translates to 'neighbourliness', a notion some call 'the very best form of evangelization.'[11]

Saskia Sassen, a renowned sociologist and globalisation ninja, points out that: 'The dominant economic narrative argues that place no longer matters ... that major industries now are information-based and hence not place-bound.'[12] She wrote this in 1994 – and noted way back then the problem with this, namely that 'economic globalization has contributed to a new geography of centrality and marginality.'

If we're not mindful of this in the digital church movement we'll end up aping it – where the educated and those with access to technological advances will see their church 'contentment' rise higher, while the financially poor and digitally disconnected on the peripheries of the mainstream will be remarginalised. The poor will then become mere objects of charitable gestures, along the lines of: 'Sure, we can't cater for them in our online gatherings or courses, but we're handing out x number of food parcels each month.' And so relationship with the marginalised gets sacrificed on the altar of reach and profile.

Wouldn't it be amazing to see many more church communities springing up that are deeply rooted in local community (and where people know each other's names), not commuted to like a shopping centre? Wouldn't it be so much more exciting to see the emergence of localised theology that isn't imported, but which listens to and speaks back into local culture?

The thing is, as the saying goes: 'Every system is perfectly designed to get the results it does.' Sadly, in many cases our models of evangelism, discipleship and spirituality have been designed with one goal in mind: to increase the number of people attending. They do that, but that's perhaps all they do, so we shouldn't be surprised when the 'bums on seats' strategy doesn't translate into transformation of lives and society.

Dallas Willard, a man of great depth and little noise, described the megachurch as: 'the swan song of a system – an economic and social system – that really has nothing to do with Christianity. It has to do with owning property, running programmes, and exercising influence in the community.'[13] He said this in an interview back in 1993, and yet today preoccupation with beating the competition, franchising and branding continues fairly unabated. How have we still not learned that these may be justifiable pursuits in business but are inappropriate primary motivators for churches?

Willard continues his critique of this logic, saying:

> Growth is understood in terms of an increase in numbers. I have never heard a church-growth advocate suggest that you might have a congregation of 55 people with no new members, no budget increase, and yet the church is growing because these people are becoming prayer powerhouses. What if spiritual growth occurs when the people who are already there grow?[14]

Measuring church growth through spiritual depth – now there's a radical idea.

Difference makers?

There's a brilliant desire in millennials to make a difference. We want our lives to count for something beyond ourselves and to impact society for the better. We value learning and self-improvement and, along with a good dollop of entrepreneurial innovation, want to use this to effect positive change in the world.

The flipside of this is that millennials can come across as entitled and fragile, overconfident and know-it-all (I'm a millennial, can you tell, lol?). Add to this a generational fatigue and suspicion towards hierarchies of power, alongside a zero tolerance for fakeness and persona, and you can see why many millennials struggle with some of the 'louder' expressions of church.

We see through the phoneyness of prosperity gospel messages that leave the poor destitute.[15] We baulk at the incongruence of lives lived not echoing sermons preached. We watch the sheer absurdity of those in public leadership peddling questionable political rhetoric behind a superficial Christian-resembling facade. We question the problematic relationship between Christian leaders and celebrity culture. We lament that the Church has taken centuries to wake up to its part in structural racism, and that even now many church leaders refute this. And we're beginning to see through the fixation with conferences throwing tired slogans our way, such as the disconcertingly aggressive promise to 'Set You On Fire'.

Part of the reason for this is that transformation is presented as a one-off event rather than a lifelong process of restoration. And the inevitable fallout is that after the initial emotional high, the event that promised so much leaves the attendee disappointed and disillusioned:

> we constantly find ourselves clinging to people, books, events, experiences, projects and plans, secretly hoping that this time it will be different. We keep experimenting with many types of anaesthetics, we keep finding 'psychic numbing' often more agreeable than the sharpening of our inner sensitivities.[16]

This is demoralising. You've spent years believing against all evidence that *this* conference will dramatically alter areas of your life you've been longing to change. But it doesn't – again. At some point you lose hope in the manufactured promises and begin to look elsewhere for answers. You oversteer from one extreme to the other and find yourself among those using the word 'deconstruction' as a badge of honour. Like many who deconstruct their faith in this way, you might become more involved with justice movements that lose sight of the perspective of the kingdom of God and replace it with left-wing rhetoric, perhaps becoming theologically progressive and socially angry. Soon advocacy for the oppressed spills into the territory of toxic dogma, dismissing any perspective different from yours and becoming discompassionate to anyone not in the same place. Ironically this ends up propagating a fundamentalist ideology and 'purity of lifestyle' we've come to recognise in the religious right, the very camp many of the deconstructionists seem to despise.

Some deconstructionists go further, seeing themselves as mavericks tasked with offending the Church. While I'm not against agitating a sleeping Church, I do think calling people *in* is infinitely preferable to calling them *out*. Gradually any sense of truth gets replaced with 'my truth' or 'your truth' – and any suggestion that there is universally knowable truth gets called 'oppressive'. 'Church' is now generally found with those who are anti-faith, and finally you hear the mantra that 'everything is prayer' – which is code for 'I don't pray anymore.' Deconstruction without renovation leads to dystopia.

We all fall short of being the people we aspire to be. God knows we do, but this type of deconstruction can bring with it an unwillingness to acknowledge that we are all hypocrites to some extent, all riddled with inconsistencies; that perhaps, though they no longer want to be 'influenced' by the Church, deconstructionists are simply being influenced by a *different* message.

Downward

So what does true influence look like that doesn't sacrifice depth for noise? I've found that the only way we can be rescued from the allure of ego-driven worldly influence is by following the humility and downward trajectory of Jesus. Our favourite academic-turned-irrelevance, Henri Nouwen, confesses his own struggle with comparison and influence:

> Despite my conscious intentions, I often catch myself daydreaming about becoming rich, powerful, and very famous. All of these mental games reveal to me the fragility of my faith that I am the Beloved One on whom God's favor rests.[17]

Going deep involves a self-emptying. This describes what a Christlike orientation to the world looks like: Jesus had every right to be 'on high' but he came 'down low'; he emptied himself of any felt entitlement to greatness; became a servant; was obedient to whatever the Father said; accepted the limitations of being restricted to a human body; subverted Satan's power games not through coercion or taking up power but through sacrifice and surrender.[18]

And how did that end? God exalted him to the highest place. Every knee in heaven and earth bows to Jesus. This downward aspiration as a kingdom value for followers of Jesus is encouraged in 1 Peter 5:6: 'Humble yourselves, therefore, under God's mighty hand, that he may lift you up in due time.' If God wants to raise your profile in the eyes of humanity, great. But the directive is for us to pursue the humility of surrender, not the noise of self-promotion. As Russell Moore reminds us: 'The kingdom came to us not from a boardroom or a literary guild, but from a feeding trough and an execution stake. Perhaps the best way to gain influence is to lose it.'[19] How do we live a life of (un)successful significance rather than meaningless influence? I believe there are five key qualities that followers of Jesus should prioritise in answer to this: depth, interest, empathy, revelation and reconciliation.

The world aims wider, the kingdom aims deeper

Jesus' way of influencing the world was not a numbers game. He wasn't at all interested in growing a 51% majority as a means to effect institutional change. Instead he invested all he had into twelve unschooled, ordinary men and a number of women (see Luke 8:1–3). Where today's culture tends to celebrate approaches that go shallow and wide like a domestic lightbulb, Jesus was absolutely focused. He went narrow and deep, like a laser. A laser consists of light beams all coming together on the same wavelength to form a beam so powerful that it can cut through metal, correct eyesight, remove tattoos or stunt hair follicle growth, to name just a few uses. A laser is much more potent than a light bulb, and yet some of our approaches to changing the world and our mindset towards how we aspire to influence people around us are more akin to the warm hue of a bedside lamp.

I believe Dallas Willard was right when he stated that God is less into counting Christians and more into weighing them. I also believe Jesus' own teaching emphasised the qualitative over the quantitative; motivation over appearance; beauty over efficiency; truth over fact; weakness over strength. So if the life of a believer is about seeking to become more like Jesus for the sake of the world around us, shouldn't we be more concerned with growing weighty in glory than with achieving lots of numerical successes? I'm aware the phrase 'growing weighty in glory' sounds like Christian jargon, but as the Hebrew word for the glory of God is כָּבוֹד (*kavod*) which comes from the root כָּבֵד (*kaved*) meaning 'heavy', there's something in Willard's language of God weighing us, as our spiritual weight or maturity reflects his glory. The kingdom of God subverts the value system of the world. In the kingdom the last are first. This is the way to the deeper things of the spirit.

The world says be interesting, the kingdom says be interested

In 1936 the eccentric British philosopher and theologian G. K. Chesterton wrote a brilliant essay called 'The Spice of Life', in which he explores how to genuinely live life well. Referencing an in thing at that moment, he wrote: 'there are a good many things in the modern world that seem to me to be dead, not to say damned, and yet are considered very spicy', for 'It seems to me that a great many people ... are at this moment paying rather too much attention to the spice of life, and rather too little attention to life.'[20]

All right – stop there. I know it all sounds a little opaque – what's he on about? Well, Chesterton gives an example to help illustrate: while he wouldn't want to ban accompanying beef with mustard, because they go so well together, he's nonetheless concerned that 'there is now a much deeper and more subtle danger that men may want to eat mustard without beef.' The danger, he says, is that we can go through life focusing on completely the wrong thing. We can turn the accompaniment into the main course and in so doing we forget about the main thing itself. We focus our pursuit on the things that are meant to enhance life but which on their own carry little value. And if we focus our energy on life's mustard rather than the beef, we'll end up feeling empty and disillusioned. For example, as 'quality of life' metrics have gone up in the West, so too have suicide and depression. Simultaneously, the 'developed' world has witnessed a huge drop in religious belief and begun to fall for the first-world problem of atheism, and some of the results are worrying levels of anxiety, mental health issues, fractured identities and purposelessness.[21]

Chesterton goes on to examine how joy cannot be drummed up by favourable external factors. You can't entertain yourself to fulfilment. That chasing after more and more 'life-changing' experiences so characteristic of my own generation of millennials becomes a mere chasing after the wind. Yet we should acknowledge this need, this instinct deep inside each of us to impress others, to be the most interesting person in the room, to be the one with the story to tell about *that* experience we had. To those of us looking to impress others with showy displays, Chesterton points us back to the glory of the mundane:

> I have experienced the mere excitement of existence in places that would commonly be called as dull as ditch-water. And by the way, is ditch-water dull? Naturalists with microscopes have told me that it teems with quiet fun … I doubt whether the fifteen gushing fountains to be found in your ornamental garden contain creatures so amusing as those the microscope reveals.[22]

He bursts the bubble that tells us we need to be noisy in order to be interesting. What would it look like for you, far from needing to gush to others about how externally successful your life is, to discover an existence that teems with quiet fun? For Chesterton this is not just important but imperative – to the extent that our survival might depend on it. For:

> there is no future for the modern world, unless it can understand that it has not merely to seek what is more and more exciting, but rather the yet more exciting business of discovering the excitement in things that are called dull.[23]

The world says knowledge, the kingdom says empathy

Knowledge can be idolised as a source of power and influence, but we tend not to care how much people know if we don't know how much they care. As Gregory the Great put it: 'the word of doctrine penetrates not the mind of one that is in need, if the hand of compassion commends it not to his heart.'[24]

Followers of Jesus need to be known not for thinking we have answers but for showing we have empathy – because empathy is the answer to every question.[25] As Romans 2:4 tells us, it's God's kindness that leads us to repentance. Not God's threat of punishment or public shaming of our sin. God's kindness. You will never influence the world for the kingdom if you cannot learn to be kind. If you receive recognition in the eyes of people for how much you know but have not learned to exhibit the kindness of God, then public acclaim will most likely be a curse not a blessing. Without kindness you can destroy with your character what you've built with your gift. Knowledge is not bad. In fact it can sometimes be very good. But without kindness, much knowledge can be dangerous.

Jesus was unimaginably kind. His kindness could destroy toxic religious paradigms in one story. His kindness could unearth age-old tradition in one demonstration.

He was *just so kind*.

The religious leaders of his day, the Pharisees, were perfect examples of those fixated with knowledge devoid of kindness. This meant that for them, rigidity prevailed over humanity, exclusivity over mutuality, the coldness of correction over the warmth of embrace. That was the religious culture in which Jesus lived. And while much of his context was worlds apart from ours, in some ways the religious aspect is not unlike the outrage-fuelled cancel culture we live in today. When someone is perceived to have put a foot out of line in the public realm, it's game over. The online mob pick up stones and start hurling them, displaying an unlikely black-and-white certainty with cries of: 'That's not the way things ought to be done!' 'We decide who is innocent and guilty!' And the disturbingly obviously ironic one, often levelled at Christians: 'You're intolerant, fundamentalist bigots!'[26]

There's a stunning story in John's Gospel of this kind of thing. You may well know it – the passage-heading at the beginning of chapter 8 often reads something like 'Woman caught in adultery' though really it should read 'Religious leaders caught with stones in their hands'. As Jesus is teaching at the temple, the Pharisees interrupt him in order to drag before him a married woman they found having sex with another man. (We aren't told why they don't also bring the man – the law states in Deuteronomy 22:22 that both the man and the woman should be put to death.) They explain the situation, expecting Jesus to join them in their outrage and hoping he'll do the cultural equivalent of writing the first condemning tweet calling for immediate public boycotting. The thing is, back then what good, law-abiding people did to show how morally superior they were to 'those' degenerates was to stone them to death. A physically violent form of cancel culture, coming from those in positions of power.

Bleurgh.

The mood immediately becomes tense as all eyes fix on Jesus. The woman collapses in a heap on the floor, sobbing, heart racing, covering her face to try and hide her shame as she awaits his verdict. And then Jesus crouches down, lowering his eye-level to hers. He bends forward. The crowd hold their breath. The woman peers through her fingers. And he begins to write, scratching his finger back and forth in the dust. We don't know what he wrote.[27] But we are told that the Pharisees continued to question him, demanding an answer to a problem they thought they knew how to handle. Then Jesus looks up at the crowd. Settling his gaze on the religious men, he offers a timeless response: 'Let any one of you who is without sin be the first to throw a stone at her' (John 8:7). And then he stoops back down and continues writing.

It's an absolute masterclass in being a non-anxious presence. But more than that, it's an exquisite example of how to de-escalate a situation while combining empathy with hard truth. Bent down on the woman's level, Jesus casts his eyes up to those looking down on them both and delivers a hug and a slap. A hug to the oppressed and a slap the oppressor.

Is the woman guilty? I guess so, if she really was cheating on her husband. Are the Pharisees right? Well no, actually. If we're using the no-quibbles Old Testament law as our guide for morality, then why do they conveniently ignore the guilty man? But that's not the question Jesus is asking. He isn't asking the 'Who is in the wrong?' question that we're so obsessed with. The question Jesus is asking is 'Which of you has the moral authority to judge others?' And, more expansively, 'Might there be a better way of doing this?'

He shows us a better way. Nowhere does he condone the actions of the woman but, equally, nowhere does he condone the actions of the Pharisees. They leave because they realise sin puts us all in the same boat, but the woman stays to wait for Jesus' final word after telling him they haven't condemned her: 'Then neither do I condemn you … Go now and leave your life of sin' (John 8:11).

Like the Pharisees, we can try to influence others with knowledge but Jesus shows us the kind of influence God admires. Jesus prioritises human empathy over religious knowledge. He speaks to our heart's motivation over our behaviour, knowing that right bodily actions follow Godly thought processes. He calls the woman out of her sin and into a new life. And thank God he does because otherwise we would all be guilty.

The world follows strategy, the kingdom follows revelation

It would be wrong to think that strategy is un-kingdom just because it's a boardroom buzzword. Strategy is good. Vision is good. But we don't want to be those who spend their lives chasing good ideas that seem clever and effective but aren't God's unique calling on us. We seek revelation and from that revelation we can devise strategy. Although the world scoffs at anyone who says they have heard God, or God revealed something to them, we must seek revelation over all else and allow strategy to emerge from that. (This is worlds apart from coming up with our own plan and asking God to bless it.)

There is a pressure to know how to adapt to the ever-changing landscape of the world around us. We're bombarded with opinions from no shortage of 'experts' offering webinars, self-help books and leadership courses. This isn't all bad (though a little overwhelming in the sheer noise of it all), though there's a real temptation to rely on confident promises to fix our problems or give us an edge in the market. But for all the good resources out there produced by well-meaning people, there are arguably even more bad resources peddled by false prophets misdiagnosing problems and mis-prescribing remedies.

Jerusalem is very close to Bethlehem – about six miles away. Yet despite geographical proximity to one another, at the time of Jesus' birth Jerusalem and Bethlehem were worlds apart. Jerusalem was a centre of trade and power, bustling with people and activity. It was a popular place of pilgrimage, with crowds flocking to the temple on important feast days. It was also where the Roman king Herod lived in a lavish palace. Power, popularity, external religious devotion, political influence – all the shiny things we're still tempted by today – are epitomised by the Jerusalem of Jesus' day. Jerusalem was where the wise men got to as they followed the star, combining their knowledge of astronomy with their devotion to truth – their strategy of science and perseverance served them pretty well. And their part in the Christmas story shows us you can come pretty close to God and his plan by honestly searching and having a good strategy. However:

> Research, study, prayer, meditation, discipline, searching, science can get you to Jerusalem; but only revelation can get you to Bethlehem. Bethlehem, with its vulnerable God in human flesh and its anticipation ... of his future suffering, is an emblem of what is unique about Christianity.[28]

Strategy can get you to Jerusalem; only revelation can get you to Bethlehem.

Jesus famously rebuked Satan, saying that humanity cannot live on bread alone but by every word that comes from the mouth of God. How do faithful followers of Jesus make sure we heed this truth rather than settling in Jerusalem, six miles away from Jesus, bloated on white sliced bread, content with the benefits of power and popularity? How do we go beyond the temptation and familiarity of relying on research, strategy and good ideas? How do we ensure we don't throw out what is unique about our faith? Avoid being both so close to but oh so far from Jesus in Bethlehem?

The answer is to prioritise God's revelation over and above any strategy.

The world categorises, the kingdom reconciles

Practically speaking, how do we get beyond noise, numbers and narcissism to having influence that is truly influential? In an increasingly divided world of tribalism and outrage, true influence will belong to those committed to helping others break out of echo chambers and to uniting disparate voices through the deep work of reconciliation.

There seem to be so many hot topics that provide ample room for disagreement these days. But we should remember that the early church was by no means free from arguments about cultural differences. In Acts 15, which took place twenty years after the initial outpouring of the Holy Spirit in Acts 2, the church was growing rapidly. With growth came diversity of culture and opinion, which caused a huge division around the issue of circumcision.

This issue simply highlighted what was already there.

Despite a powerful move of the Spirit and two decades of church growth, there was still a seemingly insurmountable wall between Jews and Gentiles. So the apostles called a council in Jerusalem to discuss the issue.

The thing is, this didn't need to be a massive dispute, as it wasn't a *realistic conflict* but simply a *cultural threat*[29] – it was just a clash between old-school Jews (who were pro-circumcision because it was what they'd been brought up to believe was honouring to God and a sign of covenant) and the new breed of Gentile believer (for whom circumcision was entirely foreign, nothing to do with their new faith in Jesus the Messiah).

Barnabas and Paul helped explain the direction the spirit of God was leading the church in closing the categories of Jew and Gentile. When they told about the miracles, signs and wonders worked through them among the Gentiles: 'The whole assembly became silent' (Acts 15:12). Presumably the silence was due to some mental recalibration as the group was convicted of how much more meaningful their broad identity as followers of Jesus was in contrast to cultural subcategories of Jew and Gentile.

It took twenty years of going into the deepest cultural loyalties of people's hearts and exposing them as less than fully true, but the Holy Spirit eventually managed to take the Acts church forward. In South Africa we're now decades post-apartheid and the Spirit is calling the Church into new territories of examining heart loyalties and cultural threats that are holding us back. But this isn't just a South African problem, it's universal. All around the world the call is for Jesus' followers to lead culture in deep engagement with local versions of historical injustices that have been left undealt with. The world needs reconciling, and if Spirit-filled believers can't lead the way, who do we expect will?

In discussing the clash that often comes from differing cultural perspectives on the past, Christena Cleveland describes two opposing world views:

> The Christian from the collectivist culture often says, 'Your people did this to my people,' whereas the Christian from the individualist culture often responds with, 'I'm not responsible for what my grandparents did.' The collectivist's socially oriented faith includes the possibility of social guilt and requires that individuals who are connected to oppressors be responsible for sins of oppression. However, the individualist's individual faith only knows individual guilt and is offended by the idea that one person can be held responsible for another person's actions.[30]

The possibility of reconciliation depends on how willing both sides are to find a middle ground. Some churches launch diversity projects to help get minorities and unheard voices speaking – but these can often end in disaster, as grappling with injustices or cultural idols tends to bring up a mess leaders weren't expecting or prepared to work through. This is to be expected, as 'diversity initiatives are doomed to fail among Christian groups that idolize their cultural identities.'[31] It's important not to throw in the towel but to allow things to develop – the *visible* mess is actually pointing to where the *hidden* mess is.

Past mess today

If you think you're good at reading, put *Vergangenheitsbewältigung* in your pipe and smoke it. *Vergangenheitsbewältigung* is a German word describing the struggle of dealing with the past. Specifically in post-war Germany, this referred to a process of denazification. South Africa desperately needs to do this – de-apartheidification, both in the seemingly small (but actually not) microaggressions of white people towards people of colour, as well as the seemingly impossible (but actually not) restitution of land and resources, to name a couple of the biggies. And other countries around the world will have their own versions of this. For example, in the UK many of the National Trust houses were funded by the slave trade. What do we do with that? Or in Canada, the Church needs to acknowledge its part in the residential school system that oppressed so many First Nation people. Recognising wrong and asking for forgiveness is empty noise if not followed by deep, restitutive action.

The ongoing plod of reconciliation:

> is often excruciating because it is the work of the cross. If reconciliation work isn't painful, I'd venture to say that it isn't really reconciliation work. Reconciliation requires that we partner with equally imperfect individuals who are also

clumsily scaling the cross-cultural learning curve, forgive those who carelessly wrong us, repeatedly ask for forgiveness, engage in awkward and unpredictable situations and, like gluttons for punishment, keep coming back for more.[32]

The only way we can keep coming back for more, without completely losing our mind and giving up, is by reminding ourselves that reconciliation work is following in Jesus' footsteps. Reconciliation cost him everything and so we should expect the same. (Could anything sound more (un)successful?) If reconciliation work feels painful, we should remember why. Hacking a path through overgrown foliage in unhospitable conditions is quite a different experience from cruising along a flat, wide road with the aircon on. But our motivation is clear: 'The desperate need of our time is not for successful Christians, popular Christians, or winsome Christians; it's for deep Christians.'[33]

I'm convinced that the move from noise to depth is one of the most needed shifts in church and culture today. No one makes this shift for the sake of popularity or approval, and it requires courage and stamina to go against the current of prevailing mindsets. On top of that, the reward for choosing to abandon the noise of a numbers-based approach is an invariable growth in engagement with local, embodied issues that cannot be solved quickly and easily. It requires us to go low and slow. But once we recognise that this is the way of the cross we are open to redefining what success may look like in relation to the Church's influence in society. There's no escaping the fact that this is hard work and will invariably bring up areas of pain in our life. What we do with the pain we experience will define the kind of person we become to those around us. That's the subject we turn to next.

Questions for reflection

1 Why do you think we find the noise of online culture so attractive?

2 What is the difference between trying to build a following versus growing in significance that really matters?

3 Who has influenced you most in your life? What aspect of their life or personality means that you are drawn to admire or perhaps even follow them?

4 This chapter touches on the kind of influence God loves: bring interested over interesting, empathy over knowledge, revelation over strategy and reconciliation over categorising. Which parts of this do you find most challenging? How can you commit to humbly following Jesus in this way?

5 How do you feel about pursuing a life of depth and reconciliation? How might you practically take steps this day, week or month to seek reconciliation in your family, work place or wider community?

4

Success is ... Transforming over transferring

What will you do with your pain?

You don't just 'treat addiction'. You end up treating anxiety, depression, PTSD, loneliness, rage, despair, toxic secrets, regret, undiagnosed head trauma, untreated ADHD. Then you realise addiction is often someone's best attempt to cope when they don't see other options.
(Dr Glenn Doyle[1])

A sum can be put right – but only by going back till you find the error and working it afresh from that point – never by simply going on. Evil can be undone, but it cannot 'develop' into good. Time does not heal it.
(C. S. Lewis[2])

I imagine that one of the reasons people cling to their hates so stubbornly is because they sense, once hate is gone, that they will be forced to deal with pain.
(James Baldwin[3])

How you deal with pain may well be the most significant factor in how your life will pan out.

The things you revert to for contentment in response to the question 'What shall I do with my pain?' will probably define the person you become. It will also define whether your pain is *transformed* into something useful, beautiful, generative, neighbour-loving (aka 'successful') or whether it's *transferred* on to others, calcifying into bitterness, sickness and broken relationships.[4] This may sound like hyperbole, but as my friend Aaron White points out:

> If you are honest, you will acknowledge that there are dark areas in your heart and mind where you have little to no control. You feel trapped and hypocritical. This interior darkness is the place where most of us have hidden our addictions.[5]

Addiction is very often a sincere attempt to solve the problem of pain but we have readily turned addiction into a moral issue, condemning those who are dependent on illegal substances as 'bad people', compounding shame in the addict and multiplying pride in ourselves. But actually we are all addicts; it's just that our 'drug of choice' – work, food, shopping, chardonnay, social media, approval of others and so on – may be more socially acceptable. The Harvard academic Arthur C. Brooks explains a little of what is going on under the surface:

> Alcoholics are addicted to alcohol, it's true. But in reality, they are hooked on what alcohol does to their brains. And so it is with workaholism. What workaholics crave isn't work per se; it is success. They kill themselves working for money, power and prestige because these are forms of approval, applause and compliments – which, like all addictive things, from cocaine to social media, stimulate the neurotransmitter dopamine.[6]

Pain can manifest in many hidden ways. Think of regrets you carry from years ago, the disappointment you feel about a particular close relationship that has turned sour or the pangs of unforgiveness you can't seem to let go of. Your pain can also play out visibly and affect you physically. Consider anxiety attacks, control issues or the inability to trust people. It's perfectly natural to seek comfort in something; it's just that in today's culture we're assaulted with a hyper-abundance of products and devices to distract us from pain and reward us for using them. All day long we carry around in our pocket the 'the modern-day hypodermic needle',[7] our smartphone, available 24/7 to administer that on-demand dopamine hit.

We rarely think to ask 'What is my need behind this behaviour? What is the emptiness I'm trying to fill here?' Western industrialised culture preys on such internal dialogue and is intentionally designed to create longing, promising to fulfil it in counterfeit ways.[8] Although we know incessant scrolling won't satisfy us, our desire for cheap hits of short-term pleasure often overrides our reason. Contrast this with the words of Psalm 103, where David instructs all his 'inmost being' to praise God, declaring that God 'satisfies your desires with good things' (Psalm 103:1, 5). God – not tech, not substances, not human affirmation, not dating apps, not a successful career.

God.

David's ancient wisdom coupled with our context points us to a consensus that is threefold: 1) We have deep inner desires that only God can satisfy but 2) we have forsaken this, searching anywhere and everywhere else for our desires to be gratified, 3) leading our inmost being to become attached to things other than God, resulting in addiction.

The well-known psychiatrist Anna Lembke tells us that as we look at successfully navigating pain, we need to be open to 'combining the science of desire with the wisdom of recovery'.[9] She points to various increased risk factors that contribute to the likelihood of turning to habits that lead to addiction: mental health issues, generational addiction in family, poverty and social upheaval. Aaron White comments: 'What many people inside and outside the church fail to see is that addictions are almost always coping mechanisms in the form of self-medicating solutions for real pain.'[10]

Our inability to process our pain successfully can lead us to look for solutions in all the wrong places. Having lived and worked over a third of my life in Manenberg, I've spent a disproportionate amount of time thinking about addiction, gang membership and the driving forces behind them. Why do certain people make such obviously destructive choices? The answer, put somewhat reductionistically, is that *pain seeks pleasure*. While never having experienced it myself, I've been told the rush heroin gives you is like receiving a long, warm hug. That sounds quite nice, doesn't it? And frankly, if I were sleeping on the streets, estranged from friends and family, and unable to deal with the trauma of, say, unrelenting sexual abuse, I would probably also turn to something whose arms were always open and from whom I need fear no judgement. I think it would be conceited to deny that many of us would do the same. Put this way, the connection between trauma and addiction is understandable.

In her disturbing memoir, *Strung Out*, Erin Khar describes her first experience of heroin as bringing 'a familiar, swift and total reprieve from the anger, anxiety, and sadness I'd felt only moments before'.[11] A miracle cure, supposedly, offering to erase any and every undesirable in our life. Sure, we all know heroin ruins lives. But we need to concede that for some, life is so terrible that to surrender to the immediate, temporary reprieve is all they can do to cope. A South African drugs policy advisor asks a poignant question about life for those living in communities to which people were forcibly removed during apartheid: 'What if, in certain circumstances, the dependent use of drugs and loyalty to a gang carried more purpose, security and meaning than any other option available?'[12] It's a sobering thought.

Now, you could be thinking: 'Oh well, I'm not from a tyrannical or particularly unjust society. I'm not on heroin and I haven't joined a gang. So I'm probably fairly immune to this.'

Unlikely.

You may not be shooting heroin nor people but you'll have learned ways to mask – for example – insecurity, fear, loneliness or despair. And as 'most of us have not learned healthy ways to deal with our pain, and we don't live in a world that encourages us to face our brokenness ... we adapt by looking for whatever we can to distract or numb us.'[13] I guarantee: you have entrenched attachments to things, people, activities or substances; you may have destructive thought patterns; you may have learned unhealthy coping mechanisms to deal with criticism or feelings of rejection. You're not alone. Every person who has ever lived has their stuff.

Today many of us are part of a generation trying to 'live our best life' but no one can tell us how, exactly. So we pretend. And then when that doesn't work we hear stuff like: 'I feel "triggered" and need to find "safe places" from "toxic positivity" to be able to "feel my feels".' And this perspective doesn't even begin to venture into the systemic, historical factors that leave whole communities at the receiving end of injustice and oppression. As the writer Resmaa Menakem points out: 'Trauma in a people, decontextualized over time, looks like culture.'[14] It's enough to trigger you into an emotional spiral. But equally, what an amazing opportunity for the Church to successfully fill a void in society and offer real hope to hurting people.

Right?

Well sure, in theory – it's just that sometimes the Church is a bit like a badly taken photo – underdeveloped and overexposed.

Underdeveloped

If the world around us seems to be struggling to know what to do with all the feels, the Church seems to have the opposite problem, tending towards ignoring emotions and the experiences that underpin them. I've even heard it taught that when an addict finds faith, they don't need rehab because *the old nature is now dead*. There's biblical precedent of course (for example, 'if anyone is in Christ, the new creation has come: the old has gone, the new is here!' (2 Corinthians 5:17)), but it can go wonky when we interpret this to mean that any attempt to work through someone's current dysfunctions caused by issues that happened pre-conversion is simply giving too much credit to the old nature and not claiming the fullness of what Jesus did on the cross. When, as I heard one well-known preacher say, to seek healing from past hurt is a 'new age tactic' aimed at making believers feel guilty for sin: 'If you're still revisiting your past it didn't help you, it made you more aware of who you're not instead of who you are.'[15]

Let me be clear: having an underdeveloped theology on how to help people deal with trauma undermines the mandate Jesus gave us to transform society. Ignoring such things can leave people in denial about what's lying under the surface, despite their having made a commitment to follow Jesus. The lack of trauma-informed culture in church, where it's unusual to talk about past pain or current attachments, can lead people to present a falsely 'sorted' persona, basically sanctifying hypocrisy. And it can cloak people in shame because they feel they're the only one still struggling with sin patterns.

This is toxic, and it's often associated with hyper charismatic theology, which in failing to acknowledge that the kingdom won't fully come until Jesus returns can lead to false promises that sin and social injustice may be completely eradicated right here right now if we have enough faith. This is something I saw first-hand in a conversation between a friend of mine and a visitor to Manenberg a few years ago. The visitor told my friend that Christians should never be sad or angry because 'God is bigger than your problems.' It left my friend feeling both a little sad and quite angry. A few short months later, the platitude-wielding visitor ended up leaving Manenberg depressed and disappointed, heartbroken by the 'lack of breakthrough' he witnessed and completely underequipped to deal with the levels of hurt and brokenness in people to whom he was ministering.

Emotional pain is rooted in history and systems too. José Humphreys, a Pastor of a multi-ethnic church in East Harlem, recognises the effects of systemic injustice on people and reflects on the brokenness of humanity as caused by collective trauma:

Our human family as a whole holds a history of wounds and trauma that come from broken exchanges between people, rooted in the breakdowns caused by sin in our world. Wounded people, wounded systems, wounding others over time and place.[16]

He goes on to explain that:

Breakdowns exist in relationship to our bodies through highly stressful environments. This is demonstrated in epigenetics, a field that researches how a person's genes can be altered by trauma, stress, and even poor diet. These can actually create constitutional changes in genes passed down to younger generations.[17]

And he maps out how big systems can cause an epigenetic altering of gene expression that leads to the ensuing disintegration of whole communities, generations later, through using the example of Holocaust survivors who transfer their PTSD to their children 'both through secondary trauma (listening to the stories of traumatized parents) and through altered genetics'.[18]

Internalised pain that works its way out personally in individuals and collectively in culture all sounds so chronic and hopeless – but as Humphreys gently reminds us: 'The collision between God's good news and our places of unraveling becomes the basis of our testimony.'[19] Has God's good news hit your place of unravelling yet? Whatever pain you carry as a human being will affect and shape you and your habits whether you like it or not.

Overexposed

One cold, damp morning during the COVID lockdown I felt God speak to me through two unremarkable scenarios. Autumn was kicking in, which meant colder weather and healthy amounts of rain. I was trying to stretch summer a little by sitting outside in the garden. As I was reading I looked up at the flower beds: bits of broken glass lying exposed on the surface of the soil caught my eye. I looked closer and could see the glint of green, brown and clear shards lying around the garden. My immediate emotion was frustration, as over the years I've spent hours and hours breaking my back digging and raking up all the old rubbish buried under the yard. Broken glass is up there with buried cat poos – very different textures but both particularly unwelcome if you're digging without gloves!

As I sat there it began to rain again and I felt God say: 'Yes, you dug deep and got rid of the broken glass, and you did a good job with what you saw. But with the rain comes a changing of the seasons.

And when it comes, it mixes up the soil again, exposing what's still buried underneath.' I realised I'd done the work for summer – I'd found and rooted out many rocks, stones, bits of old food packaging, various plastics and a lot of broken glass buried in the soil. But now autumn was coming and it revealed what remained unseen in summer through the rain turning the soil. And I considered how true this is for my inner pain.

As I seek to dig deep through my damaged soul I remove the brokenness I'm aware of by handing it over to Jesus, and turn from it in repentance and a renewed mind. But I can only deal with what I'm aware of. When the seasons in life change, new issues are often brought to the surface and various sin patterns or negative thoughts or habits are exposed that we hadn't noticed before – which gives us a new opportunity to dig deep and root out all that's not good soil. And we're then able to thrive – body, soul and spirit – in the same ground but in a new season. Our view towards the broken glass transforms from one of frustration to realising that allowing it to come up was the kindest thing God could do for us.

I wonder, though, if the Church isn't generally ill-equipped to deal with the exposing of our issues. There seems to be a steady stream of stories of overexposed church leaders caught in financial scandals, affairs, abuse and toxicity. I'm not here to condemn, but we've got to ask whether this is a sign that church culture, far from having solutions for peoples' pain, is actually being formed and led by a disproportionate number of people unable to break out of their own cycles of addictions and attachments. Where such church culture encourages us simply to polish the surface of our lives to look clean and presentable, Jesus invites us to get dirty, digging in the earth and pulling up roots. This is hard work and takes time. But we have to go there because: 'We cannot begin to help others if we do not take this work seriously in our own lives.'[20]

The very same afternoon, I was doing some carpentry in the garden when a member of our Tree of Life community, Preswin, walked past me and tried to open the door of the storage room, managing to break the handle right off. My immediate emotion was frustration – if he only knew how many times I'd had to replace that handle. As we looked for another in the various drawers in the storeroom, I felt the Lord speak again: 'See how boring it gets replacing the same handle? Frustrating going round and round with the same issue, isn't it? Thing is, unless you get to the root of the problem, no number of new handles will solve it.' I actually knew what the root issue was but hadn't done anything about it. The door was always difficult to lock because the position of the striking plate in the frame was slightly off. So you'd instinctively pull harder on the handle to try and align the lock, resulting in lots of broken handles. While we obviously needed to replace the handle, to fix the problem for good we really needed to enable the lock to engage properly. I began to think about the specific issues in my life that I get tired of coming up again and again; might it be that we get so used to trying to solve an issue by replacing the handle again, all the while ignoring the actual driver of the problem? What if, when our heart next sinks due to our familiar 'below-the-line' behaviour that we're aware of but seemingly can't escape, we take time to sit with Jesus and together discern what the root is, rather than assuming we know?

As we look to transforming our pain successfully rather than transferring it on to others, we'll need to learn that freedom lies not just in an initial breakthrough moment but in the ensuing follow-through journey. Let me explain.

Then what?

I once heard a story of an itinerant evangelist who was travelling through the city in which friends of mine lived. Over lunch one day the travelling minister laid out his power credentials as he relayed to my friends that the previous evening twenty-seven addicts were totally set free and delivered from addiction – all in one meeting. As my friends retold the story they shared how inadequate they felt listening to these impressive stats. They'd been labouring in the same mission field for years, and what others claimed to have seen in a matter of hours had taken them decades. If seeing people set free from addiction really was as straightforward as channelling a more powerful anointing of the Holy Spirit in a once-off evening meeting, then why had they bothered with the long, hard, uphill slog of walking alongside the hurting and addicted the last thirty years?

Hearing their wrestle was so refreshing. Many conversations, or testimonies of instant deliverance of addicts and immediate, pain-free breakthroughs, have fuelled a sense of failure or futility in my own heart towards our approach. A lot of the time, in my experience, these 'changed people' are not as deeply changed as the testimony about them claims. This isn't to say God hasn't touched them or that they haven't encountered the Holy Spirit in some way, simply that the Christian life isn't just a one-time event. Salvation involves having an encounter leading to a choice; but faithfully following Jesus after that involves making choices that lead to encounters. It's full of many events and celebrations – yes, for sure, when someone makes an initial commitment to follow Jesus but also when they continue to choose him despite navigating the desolation of grief or crisis; when they hold on to him despite life going in the opposite direction to the spine-tingling prophecies they received early on; when, though they might be struggling to find passion for Scripture, a steady discipline is etched on their heart and they continue to submit themselves to it knowing that though they may not feel anything, somehow it is true; or when, despite decades of faith-filled prayer, the healing they seek doesn't come, but on the other side of disappointment they learn a new depth of worship and intimacy. Might these be as worthy of celebration as an initial verbal commitment to Jesus, the connotations of which, in that moment, may not have been truly grasped?

My friends' main point when relaying this story was: 'Great, but then what?'

Even if those twenty-seven addicts did get free from chemical dependence in that moment, what was the plan for walking with them for the rest of their lives? What was the vision for their discipleship – including helping them work through all the issues and pain that got them to the point of addiction? So often in the Gospels, when people believe in Jesus or are healed, we don't actually hear about how the rest of their lives went. The woman at the well with five husbands in John 4 – were all her relationship issues instantly sorted when she became an evangelist to her village after her initial encounter with Jesus? Did the deep pain she felt suddenly melt away? Did the habits and methods of coping she'd learned instantly dissipate or did it take time for her to remind herself of her new identity as a dearly loved daughter of God? We just aren't told. Or what about the demoniac in Mark 10? After he was healed, are we to believe he never had any more problems? Did he weep over the memories of years he spent abandoned, chained up in a graveyard, self-harming – or was this miraculously erased? Did he ever relapse? How did he navigate the social dynamic with villagers who continued to shun him in the marketplace? We just don't know.

What we do know is that even the apostles, as they saw miracles and revival break out around them, battled with personal issues (arguments, doubts and disagreements), opposition (you know, just minor things like riots, trials and stonings) and were so hated that many of them were killed for their faith. The point is, initial breakthrough from sin and dysfunction isn't the *end* of the story, it's the *beginning*.

If the Church is going to embrace and walk alongside broken people there are no shortcuts. We're told in 1 John 3:16 that 'Jesus Christ laid down his life for us. And we ought to lay down our lives for our brothers and sisters.' Laying down your life for others is the call of discipleship. If we want to partner with the Holy Spirit in bearing fruit that *truly lasts* (rather than some short-term stats that gradually fizzle out), we need to recognise that once-off evangelism events are inadequate in and of themselves to bring that about.

And so with broken lives – each of ours, yes, but especially those that have been unbearably painful – there is no other option than to go back to the past and methodically help heal the wounds of a lacerated soul. It's slow, it's deliberately quiet, which is why many don't have time for it – but it points to the kind of success to which Jesus calls his followers.

Jesus did it

What this looks like will vary for each of us, and in John 21 we read a beautiful example of Jesus leading Peter through his own process of inner healing. This is the third time Jesus appears to his disciples post-resurrection. They'd gone back to fishing, back to their old lives. Uncertain how to move on past the trauma of watching Jesus executed, perhaps they'd relapsed or maybe they just returned to familiar behavioural patterns. They'd tasted heaven for three years, witnessed countless miracles, sat at the feet of Jesus and heard every parable and teaching he ever gave – and yet when disappointment struck, they found themselves afraid of what the future held and went straight back to what they knew, back to their old lives. We all tend to retreat in this way. Thankfully, Jesus is patient.

At dawn one morning Jesus breaks into the disciples' lives again. They'd been fishing all night but caught nothing. Exhausted and frustrated, they must have rolled their eyes and let out various expletives when a strange figure on the beach started shouting directions to them on how to catch fish. 'Throw your net on the right side of the boat and you will find some' (John 21:6). Such basic advice – as though they hadn't been doing that continually for the last few hours! But devoid of any better ideas, they heed this know-it-all's advice and achieve in an instant what they'd failed to the whole night.

There's a beautiful parallel here, a symmetry between this post-resurrection story and a similar story in Luke 5. In both cases Jesus enables a miraculous catch of fish, but in the Luke story this happens before the disciples have got to know him and have a grid for his miracles. So in Luke, when Jesus instructed them to let down the nets, they'd probably have reacted as we imagined they did in John's story – sighing in frustration, aching from physical exhaustion. But they did then let down the nets and caught so many fish that the boat almost sank. So extraordinary was it that one last try would result in such a huge haul after catching nothing all night, that Peter immediately reacted with a mix of incredulity and conviction. Dropping to his knees he said to Jesus: 'Go away from me, Lord; I am a sinful man!' (Luke 5:8). He hadn't the capacity to bear the shame of his sinfulness in such proximity to Jesus' holy power – perhaps mirrored by the nets themselves breaking under the weight of the fish.

For all the similarities in the two passages, there's one notable difference. In John, at Peter's point of revelation, as he recognises this miracle as a hallmark of the one he loved so much, his instinct is completely rewired. Rather than feeling condemned and putting distance between himself and Jesus as he had previously, he now dives into the water fully clothed, swims frantically to shore and embraces Jesus with utter joy. Later we read that the catch totalled 153 fish, meaning they must have counted each one. There must have been something quite comical in their checking the nets over and over and seeing this time that none had broken, and their sighs of relief, the weight lifted from their weary shoulders.

The memory of the last three years was indelibly engraved in the deepest parts of Peter's heart. He just knew Jesus would embrace him despite how he'd let him down. And even though Peter had returned to his old life, the depth of love he had for Jesus had never disappeared. Simply put, it was time with Jesus *over a number of years* that changed Peter's heart from shameful fear to sheer delight. He had to be patient. Time with Jesus takes – time.

So Peter had got to shore. You can imagine him hugging Jesus, soaking him and laughing. Overjoyed. Dripping. Safe. Seen. Relieved. Jesus had a fire on the go on which to make breakfast. And that's when Peter smells the smoke wafting through the morning breeze – and he freezes. In an instant he spirals back into traumatic memories he can't shake off of that time just recently when he was sitting around a fire and denied Jesus three times. It all comes flooding back. Shame returns: 'One of the hardest things for traumatized people is to confront their shame about the way they behaved during a traumatic episode.'[21] He goes silent as he stares into the red coals. Jesus hands out fish and bread; this triggers Peter again. He replays things in his head: that time Jesus fed thousands of people with one boy's lunch; the kindness of God towards people in need; the disciples handing out fish and bread; the multiple baskets of leftovers. Guilt sweeps over Peter as he wonders how he could have betrayed his friend like that. He remains silent and hardly eats.

By now the others have noticed something is not quite right with their friend, who is usually so loud and extroverted. Jesus looks his way and addresses him directly. He knows something is wrong. Peter was living with a specific, deep wound. Essentially, he is blaming himself for Jesus' crucifixion. If only he'd stood up for Jesus being falsely accused, maybe he could have helped avert the gruesome pain his friend went through. But Jesus knows all about it, doesn't hold it against him and doesn't judge him for it. In fact in the same way he does for each one of us, Jesus had a unique process of healing just for his dear friend Peter.

I imagine him putting his arm around Peter and the two of them walking along the beach a little. And then Jesus asks Peter if he loves him – a weird way of initiating a conversation and one that comes across a little insecure. But he does it twice more – and by the third time Peter is hurt. He exclaims: 'Yes, Lord, you know that I love you.' He resents Jesus' questioning. But then I wonder if the penny drops and Peter realises that, with his answer of similar force to the one he gave when he denied knowing Jesus, he has now affirmed his love for his friend in a way that, in its threefold symmetry, 'undoes' each of his previous three denials.

I don't know what your template is for demonic deliverance, but this is a beautiful deliverance – a continuation of Peter's inner healing process. The internal transformation has huge social connotations. There is empirical change in him – he goes from wet blanket in the face of pressure from a few onlookers, to rock on which the Church is built when he later stands firm under pressure from religious and political authorities.

But then Jesus says something strange about Peter's future: 'when you are old you will stretch out your hands, and someone else will dress you and lead you where you do not want to go' (John

21:18). John writes that Jesus was foretelling how Peter would die. It's unclear whether Peter registered this in the moment, but his response is revealing. He sees John and asks 'Lord, what about him?' He still seems bound by insecurity and comparison. Jesus replies: 'If I want him to remain alive until I return, what is that to you? You must follow me' (vv. 21–22).

Peter ended up being martyred in AD 65 under the Emperor Nero. Jesus had essentially prophesied what would happen to him: he was executed by crucifixion. What's the point? Neither being martyred in the prime of life nor living to old age are the point. The point is: *as for you, you must follow me.* Each of us has our unique individual calling and will require our unique individual healing to fulfil it. That doesn't mean we should wait until we're all sorted – we'll never be all sorted. But Peter's story shows us that in a symmetrical symbiosis, healing happens as calling unfolds; calling happens as healing unfolds. Fast-forward a couple of weeks after this exchange to Pentecost. As the fire of the Spirit is falling all around, Peter preaches a knockout message to cynics and critics – and ushers in *the* moment on which the Church was built.

The wet blanket had finally become the rock.

What about you? Do you struggle with feeling ashamed? Traumatised? Aimless? Struggling with comparison? Relapsing on old lies and behaviours? What would God have to say to you? If this story tells us anything it is that he is saying: 'I can use all of that!' He did it with Peter and he wants to do it with you. The very things you think are your weaknesses can be transformed into strengths. As you journey on in your process of learning to be (un)successful, this is one of the counter-intuitive secrets of the kingdom of God.

Getting practical

I've come to believe there is no *true* healing from addiction except through finding the ability to transform the pain it's trying to mask through the redemptive power of Jesus' death and resurrection. Only through this power – what AA famously calls 'higher power' – will anyone be able to break truly free from the past and walk, however tentatively, into Jesus' promise of new life.

I'm all for counselling (I've seen a psychologist in various seasons of my life) and, when needed, medication; and I absolutely believe in the importance of a crossover of theology and the social sciences. I also believe it's possible for someone struggling with addiction to get clean and stay sober without any reference to faith in Jesus. But for humanity's deepest, most primal pain, I truly believe that ultimately only Jesus' love can redeem it into beauty. Not a one-off prayer or conversion but something much more beautiful. The story of some of what my wife, Sarah, has been through illustrates this well.

In the second year of running Cru62, a young man we were sharing our home with and who had become like a son to us was tragically killed in a car accident. Maruwaan, who had come to faith in Jesus after being miraculously delivered of heroin addiction, was twenty-one years old when he died and had only just begun to taste what 'life in its fullness' was like. His sudden death sparked off a chain reaction of trauma from Sarah's past. As a child she experienced the loss of five of her friends, three of whom were killed violently. As a student she witnessed the death of her sister, grandmother and mother within the space of two years, and then a few years later her father died by suicide. That is a lot of death for someone to experience by the age of thirty-two. Sarah was left with a lot of grieving and processing to do. And before she could even begin to come to terms with the more recent tragedies she had to go back to the beginning and work her way forward in what would become a long process of inner healing. What followed was a journey of unearthing layers of emotional wounds, spiritual doubt, psychological trauma, neurological damage and physiological pain, and discovering multi-faceted approaches to dealing with each of these different aspects of her experience of loss. She spent time at a Christian inner-healing retreat centre where the emotional wounds were prayed through as the Holy Spirit brought memories to light. She journalled her crises of faith in a loving God who would apparently allow such tragedy, writing into the small hours of the night as she gave full expression to her doubts and questions. She saw a psychologist for therapy, counselling and eating plans to promote healthy brain function. She did neuro-feedback to restore neurological pathways and retrain synapses. And she discovered TRE (Trauma Release Exercises) to tap into and release the physical storing of trauma in the body.

It was this last intervention in particular that fascinated us because it seemed to bring together scientific research and spiritual manifestation. In short, TRE helps release deep muscular patterns of tension and trauma through activating a natural reflex mechanism of shaking that releases muscular tension.[22] To an onlooker it simply looks like a room of people lying on the floor shaking, and sometimes crying or laughing uncontrollably – not dissimilar to a charismatic church gathering. In Sarah's process of healing, we discovered that the very means the Holy Spirit has been using for millennia to set people free from pain and trauma were also being practised by those coming at healing from a scientific angle. It greatly increased our trust in both perspectives.

Sarah's journey was personal to her and by no means exhaustive – there are plenty of other ways to assist our healing processes. But at the heart of all of this was the conviction that any approach devoid of Jesus' presence is inadequate to make us free. He is the healer and can breathe his life into any approach humanity comes up with to heal our pain.

Lockdown deliverance

When the hard COVID lockdown was announced in South Africa in March 2020, Sarah and I felt it would be a golden opportunity to invest in vulnerable people's lives for a few weeks. We decided to offer a place to stay to a number of friends in Manenberg who were at various stages of recovery from addiction or had complicated home environments. Two of the hallmarks of that time were the level of conflict that came up between us all and the depth of inner healing many of us experienced. One particular scenario comes to mind.

An argument that had been brewing for weeks suddenly exploded between two of the people in the group; a third person, Waydin, found himself caught in the middle. In the past, Waydin had learned to deal with such scenarios through violence and crystal meth. But now, as a follower of Jesus, he knew violence wasn't ultimately the answer but still sometimes struggled to know how to process the extreme emotions he felt.

Sarah and I sent the rest of the group to the prayer room and sat with Waydin. As we chatted things through, Waydin's face started tightening up and his body language became more extreme as he began aggressively gesticulating what he was going to do to the friend he felt was in the wrong. Then he flipped. Jumping up off the sofa and running out of the front door, he sprinted towards the prayer room, shouting and breaking stride only to pick up bricks along the way and hurl them in the direction of the other guys. I got to the prayer room seconds after him to find him grabbing one of the guys by the neck. I jumped on him and we fell to the ground as I wrapped my arms around his to try and release the pressure he was exerting on his friend's neck. We eventually prized Waydin off him. Finally Sarah came in and began praying out loud. As she started shouting 'In the name of Jesus, come out of him!', Waydin's eyes rolled back into his head and looked as though they darkened. He continued to threaten the others and his face started contorting as if he was having a seizure. Eventually we got everyone out of the prayer room apart from ourselves and another volunteer, and Waydin came back to himself. He began to be able to regulate his breathing but every now and then would try and break free and start shouting, only to slump back down again, crying. We repeated over him that he was loved, he was safe and that he needn't be afraid. And we sat there for half an hour or so, gently affirming him and praying in tongues.

Later, chatting with Sarah, I realised we had just witnessed a demonic manifestation and that we probably needed to have a go at deliverance. So we laid hands on Waydin, prayed in tongues and commanded whatever it was to leave him. Nothing much happened. It was only when we got Waydin himself to pray – acknowledging his pain, repenting for his violent outburst and asking Jesus to take it from him – that a heaviness lifted and the room was filled with peace. Over the course of the next few months I helped Waydin work through some of the trauma of his childhood and ask the Holy Spirit for revelation on things he may not have known about or had forgotten about, to give over to God.

Neither healing nor deliverance are guarantees of a problem-free life. Even after the Holy Spirit has worked in your heart you can choose whether to partner with the healing or with brokenness. Both Sarah's and Waydin's stories continue to work themselves out.

Some days are better than others – such is life. But pivotally, both continue to lean into the presence of God, pressing into relationships of loving accountability, finding their place in community, having come to recognise that there are no quick fixes to protracted pain.

We've all got pain. The question is what you'll do with yours. Will you transfer it on to others or hand it to God for him to transform? If you do – if you allow him into your pain – your deepest worldly loss could well become your greatest eternal victory.

Questions for reflection

1 What do you think about the idea of everyone carrying pain? What are your go-to coping mechanisms for dealing with pain, disappointment or fear? Have you ever transferred your pain on to others?

2 Have you ever experienced God transforming an area of pain or trauma in your life into something redemptive?

3 What are areas of collective trauma in your home culture and where do you think they came from?

4 What attachments or addictions could you invite Jesus to help you with?

5 Do you agree with the assertion that the Church is underdeveloped in addressing trauma? Why might this be and how could it be changed?

5

Success is ... Being a faithful presence in the culture wars
Why the kingdom is inherently political

Jesus was not killed by atheism and anarchy. He was brought down by law and order allied with religion, which is always a deadly mix ... Beware those who cannot tell God's will from their own.
(Barbara Brown Taylor[1])

I learned long ago never to wrestle with a pig. You get dirty, and besides, the pig likes it.
(Anon.)

For every civilization, for every period in history, it is true to say: 'Show me what kind of a god you have, and I will tell you what kind of a humanity you possess.'
(Emil Brunner[2])

We've looked at our own tendency to pursue worldly calling, relevance and influence over God's definition of success, but how does this play out for the body of Christ on a societal level? What kind of Church are we aiming to be? How does this define our cultural engagement? What are we 'for' and 'against', and can we give credible reasons for our stance? And how can a perspective of (un) success help us play our part in restoring credibility to the Church and representing Jesus to the world more faithfully?

I first came across the term 'moral ecologies' when reading a book called *The Second Mountain* by David Brooks, columnist on *The New York Times*. He explains that:

> We all grew up in one moral ecology or another. We all create microcultures around us by the way we lead our lives and the vibes we send out to those around us. One of the greatest legacies a person can leave is a moral ecology – a system of belief and behavior that lives on after they die.[3]

Put simply, a moral ecology consists of the collective factors – such as your family, education, religion – that form us and from which we then shape and influence the world around us. These moral ecologies don't just encompass an individual's effect on their personal world, they can 'define whole eras and civilizations … Moral ecologies are collective responses to the big problems of a specific moment.'[4] Brooks uses the example of mid-twentieth-century European 'collectivism', where a shared interest in surviving the Nazi threat motivated populations to limit their individual choice or expression, voluntarily deferring to authority. Then, when this threat dissipated, the wartime moral ecology was gradually replaced in the 1960s by an openness to self-expression, individualism and the rejection of conformity to – what was seen as – dogmatic conservatism. The debate continues as to whether this cultural revolution was a harmful time of loose morals and sin or a liberating time of unbridled creative expression. My point is simply this: we're at a point in the history of the Church's role in the world at which we need a new collective approach – call it a 'kingdom moral ecology' – to respond successfully to the big problems of this specific moment in time.

We need to rethink what collective factors form us as followers of Jesus, and what faithful witness entails to a generation that, lacking any seeming awareness of God's activity in the world, are simultaneously obsessed, and utterly bored with, themselves. And my conviction is that a Spirit-infused antidote to this is for Jesus' followers to live lives marked by moral ecologies of God's supernatural power coupled with wise discernment, along with a generosity of spirit to participate in the suffering of others.

In relating Jesus' life and teaching on the kingdom of God to today's culture wars, there's no escaping that what we witness going on around us, within and without the Church, is concerning. The seeming lack of ability to display common decency in the public sphere – to first listen, to *empathise*, to seek to understand and to demonstrate kindness face to face (and especially online, where the guarantee of anonymity fuels the vitriol) – is dramatically antithetical to what Jesus preached. Both in the Gospels generally and the Beatitudes in particular, followers of Jesus are given an alternative way of being in the world. And the way of the kingdom is always counter to the powers at play in prevailing culture. Following Jesus was no less subversive 2,000 years ago than it is now.

So as we begin this chapter navigating a minefield, we would do well to remind ourselves that Jesus taught us to celebrate meekness (simply defined as 'power willingly restrained' – could any characteristic be more needed?), to be peacemakers and to embrace persecution and misunderstanding. He celebrated vulnerability and welcomed children, he embraced women as his equal and spent most of his time with those who possessed no power for him to use to leverage influence. He healed everyone who came to him, not just those who 'got' him or agreed with his teaching. He chose disciples from politically opposed camps and formed a community with them, turning them from partisans to penitents. Jesus coupled supernatural power with wise discernment and displayed a generosity of spirit to participate in the suffering of others. He is the God we claim to represent, and so he is our example to follow.

The politics of religion?

Nowhere did Jesus tell his followers to fight for political power or even religious freedom. And in fact the early church thrived despite – or maybe because of – persecution and the coercion of empire. It was only when the Emperor Constantine declared Christianity the state religion that political supremacy co-opted the gospel and the church jumped into bed with military force and was drained of its prophetic power-from-below.

It is my belief that it's impossible to follow Jesus faithfully and for your faith *not* to influence every area of your life. This includes your politics. And if you call yourself a Christian, then your political views should be centred on love over anything else. And while faith and politics must necessarily interact, we need to recognise that politics is concerned only with this world here and now whereas a kingdom moral ecology is about transforming this world through the sure promise of another world breaking in. Eugene Peterson explains:

> A person has to be thoroughly disgusted with the ways things are to find the motivation to set out on the Christian way. As long as we think the next election might eliminate crime and establish justice or another scientific breakthrough might save the environment … we are not likely to risk the arduous uncertainties of the life of faith. A person has to get fed up with the ways of the world before he, before she, acquires an appetite for the world of grace.[5]

The majority of the people alive today do not know about this world of grace but instead fixate on individual striving for achievement.

Brooks adds: 'People who are left naked and alone by radical individualism do what their genes and the ancient history of their species tell them to do: They revert to tribe. Individualism, taken too far, leads to tribalism.'[6] He defines tribalism in two steps: it offers 'connection based on mutual hatred' and so becomes a 'community for lonely narcissists'.[7] And the problem with tribalism? It 'is asking more from politics than politics can deliver'.[8]

At least in part the tension between politics and faith seems to be that we're attempting to relate an unseen, timeless reality – the kingdom of God – to a visible, temporary state of affairs. When heaven meets earth the shockwaves reverberate into every sphere of society and, as we'll see, politics is no exception. First, we need to consider some distinctions.

What politics is

Politics is primarily concerned with the power relations and governance of countries or states through the distribution of resources, for the flourishing of humanity (pretty simple actually; just really hard to do well).

What politics isn't

It isn't simply an us-versus-them propaganda war of populist media personalities launching personal attacks on opponents by digging for dirt on them or their family. Nor is it an avenue to personal betterment through nepotism. Nor is it an inherently 'dirty' pursuit.

What the gospel is

The gospel is good news announced by Jesus' life, death and resurrection. It centres on the truth that God's kingdom has broken into the sin-tainted systems and structures of the world and is making all things new. Far from exclusive, it is the most inclusive thing ever – you just have to opt in to be part of it.

What the gospel isn't

It's not a message only concerned about getting disembodied souls to heaven. (If that's all there is to it, let the forests burn, don't worry about the ice caps and racial oppression, poverty, modern-day slavery – none of it's important compared to getting souls into heaven because there everyone will be happy and sorted. All right, I'm getting carried away...)

Culture wars

A culture war is a conflict about a polarising issue between different perspectives, generally between conservatives and progressives and played out publicly in political and social life.

Our job as Jesus followers is to work out how to bring the kingdom of God successfully into every structure and sphere of society.[9] We are all theologians and politicians – even if you hate God and political debate – and who you understand Jesus to be, through the lens of your moral ecology, will dictate how you think the Church should operate in the political sphere.

Theology *needs* politics. But this is not a one-way street. Politics *needs* theology.

Christians have so often taught that the political is unspiritual but this means the Church misses out on our serving the world. To say you're unpolitical is itself a political statement – and one that inherently supports injustice, by the way. That's because without the wise ordering of power in society, anarchy ensues, and if a state of anarchy means that 'bullies (economic or social as well as physical) will always win, [and] therefore the weak and vulnerable will always need protecting', then can't we see that 'social and political structures of society are part of the creator's design'?[10] Elizabeth Phillips explains:

Our political opinions and practices will inevitably be shaped and guided by claims about truth, what is good and what is ultimate. If we are not intentional about allowing our politics to be guided by what is truly ultimate in Christianity, we find instead that our politics are conformed to ideologies which claim that something other than the triune God is ultimate. The Christian church has always called such claims idolatry.[11]

The missiologist Hans Hoekendijk pointed out that the word 'ekklesia was, from the very beginning, a "theo-political" category'.[12] And so mission is to be concerned with the social, economic and political conditions in this world, not simply growing big congregations. We will only be able to partake in this mission of God 'successfully' if we are continually interrogating our own judgementalism and offering love to a hurting world.

Why I am in the same boat as a drug dealer

Judging people can feel good. We all do it to some extent, the only difference is the varying targets we choose (for example, meat eaters might be judged by some as contributing to global warming and the destruction of rainforests, and vegans as contributing to global warming and the destruction of soil biota). It's a pretty exhausting way to spend our time, yet the outrage culture isn't new. However, what this culture largely fails to recognise is the reality, ultimately quite freeing, that we're *all* hypocrites.

None of us live up to the ideals we profess.

If the very thing you criticise in others is not something you specifically struggle with, fair enough, but there are probably plenty of other things you do that are just as damaging for society. C. S. Lewis inconveniently reminds us that: 'If you think you are not conceited, it means you are very conceited indeed.'[13] We're all complicit, in some way, in the people, issues or systems we rally against. If you ask a drug dealer whether they think selling drugs to children is a good way to live, they'll likely answer in the negative and then seek to justify why they do it anyway. I've had many conversations with drug dealers that go along similar lines:

'So do you think selling drugs to children is a good career choice? Getting them addicted from the age of thirteen, so they have to commit crimes or sell their bodies to continue using your product?'
'No, it's not a good thing I'm doing.'
'So why do you keep doing it?'
'Because there are no jobs, and my own kids and family need to eat, need clothes, school supplies. That sort of thing.'
'Right, but can't you see that enslaving other people's children into addiction so that you can feed your own is pretty hypocritical?'
'Yes, but at least I don't rob people or shoot people with guns.'
'No, but you're still breaking down society by your choices.'
'Listen, I don't force anyone to buy drugs – I just sell them to whoever wants them. If I didn't sell drugs, they'd just go down the road to another merchant. So what difference does it make? *I'm just one person among many all doing the same thing.*'

I want to suggest there's less room to judge this drug dealer than we might at first imagine because the rationale they use is pretty typical of most non-drug-dealing citizens. Maybe the following conversation helps explain:

'So do you think it's all right that the factory workers who assembled your smartphone in China are working in unjust conditions?'

'No, it's not all right.'

'So why do you keep buying electronic devices?'

'I don't really have any other options. I require a smartphone
    for my job, to pay the bills and put food on the table for my
    family.'

'Right, but can't you see that contributing to the enslavement
    of desperate people in other parts of the world, just so you
    can feed your family, is pretty hypocritical?'

'Yes, but at least I don't work for an oil company or tobacco
    manufacturer.'

'No, but you're still affecting humanity and the world nega-
    tively by your choices.'

'Listen, I'm not to blame here. Even if I didn't have a smart-
    phone others would keep buying them. *I'm just one person
    among many all doing the same thing.*'

Despite standing for complete opposites, both the secular left
and the religious right tend to operate along the same lines.
Neither side allows for nuance, diversity of opinion or even
the notion that other perspectives have something to offer. The
secular left conceptualises love through lifting up the oppressed
before they die, the religious right conceptualises love by saving
people from damnation after they die. To trample love underfoot
in the name of being right is never right, whichever side you're
coming from. Trying to live out a kingdom moral ecology today
will necessarily have political connotations because politics is
how humans order power – and a redemption of power is at the
heart of the kingdom. We must strive to keep the kingdom of
God at the centre of it all. But when either the left or the right
try to co-opt the kingdom for political means, it ceases to be the
kingdom.

Against or absent?

In many ways the Church in the West has failed to engage successfully with culture wars playing out around us by either posturing
ourselves against society or retreating from the political debate
altogether. For example (in my opinion), concerning debate over
abortion the Church seems to engage readily with politics but over
climate disaster nowhere near readily enough. We seem to lack a
coherent theological foundation for faithful witness.

If my borderline-unhealthy social-media scrolling has shown me
anything, it's that the Church's social-media presence is often rather
self-centred. The clinical psychologist Meg Jay writes of a mentality
today whereby we aim to build our unique 'identity capital'[14] by
weighing up the merits of different hobbies and pursuits, choosing
those we think will make us seem more interesting. But as Brooks
says, while 'each individual day is fun ... it doesn't seem to add up to
anything'.[15] We can apply this to well-known Christian celebrities or
churches. From soundbite clips from a Sunday sermon and photos
of happy-looking people with hands in the air, to an occasional
nod to some topical issue or a monochrome photo advertising an
album launch, it all looks quite fun but doesn't amount to much. If
we're not careful we'll begin to rate our Christian life by racking up
social-media-worthy experiences at the risk of missing the beauty
of the un-photo-worthy plod of faithfulness and obedience: 'Living
online often means living in a state of diversion. When you're living
in diversion you're not actually deeply interested in things; you're
just bored at a more frenetic pace.'[16]

What does (un)success look like in navigating the shifting sands
of cultural engagement? Are Christians as frenetically bored as
anyone else? And if we are, what can we do about it? How can the
Church avoid either simply judging culture or just staying silent on

the framing issues of our day and promoting anaemic Christian content?

Snakes and doves

Far from trying to assimilate to mainstream culture, Jesus used jarring cultural juxtapositions to convey aspects of the kingdom he was preaching about. His choice of disciples shows this, as do the words he told them as he sent them out into a world where he knew many people would never fully understand them. His advice to them was to be wise as snakes and innocent as doves. Snakes and doves have very little in common – yet together they point to a combination of attributes that, if drawn together, Jesus said would yield positive results. As Martin Luther King (MLK) said, 'life at its best is a creative synthesis of opposites in fruitful harmony.'[17]

MLK goes on to describe this combination as the tough mind and the tender heart. That is the opportunity of holding together and even blending 'strongly marked opposites'[18] – representing a third way – for rather than closing down diversity of opinion it opens up discussion and generates new possibilities beyond two binary options. For MLK, the tough mind is one that is able to see through false claims of truth or fulfilment and show a 'firmness of purpose and solidness of commitment' in the face of 'easy answers and half-baked solutions'.[19]

A big consideration in navigating culture wars today, where easy answers and half-baked solutions are no less common, is where we go for our news. What voices do we trust and how do we discern hidden agendas? Why is it, for example, that evangelical Christians tend to be disproportionately susceptible to believing and spreading conspiracy theories, fake news and fringe opinions? I think it has something to do with the influences on many Christians.

The contemporary evangelical world view is generally formed by a combination of political conservatism, negative orientation towards 'the world', scepticism towards science and academia, alongside dubious ideas around spiritual authority, often resulting in uncritical loyalty to a small selection of celebrity pastors and their teachings. Sure, this is a stereotype, but allowed to develop unchecked it can become a brittle, black-and-white, confrontational us-versus-them attitude when brought into the public sphere. As such, the fruit tends to be counterproductive arguments fuelling polarity, as opposed to constructive debate energising understanding. The Christian imagination loses its curiosity when the answers to life's biggest questions can only be viewed as 'against' so many things in culture. This becomes what MLK describes as softminded. He remarks:

> The softminded man always fears change. He feels security in the status quo and has an almost morbid fear of the new … The softminded person always wants to freeze the moment and hold life in the gripping yoke of sameness.[20]

And continues: 'Softmindedness is one of the basic causes of racial prejudice … Race prejudice is based on groundless fears, suspicions, and misunderstandings.'[21] It would be softminded of us to ignore, for example, the structural and historic oppression of people of colour by white people. Failing to address this huge issue due to a fear of the new, finding comfort in the status quo, freezing progress, gripping tightly to 'the way we've always done it' – too often this is what the Church represents to wider culture, and it is a disastrous moral ecology to be known for and pass down to the next generation.

And yet a cursory look into the life of the early church in Acts or Paul's epistles shows an agitating, disruptive church that brought dynamic change to the religious structures and political status quo and challenged the assumptions of traditional mindsets. Those early followers of the Way, far from excluding people based on race or ethnic heritage, were led by the Holy Spirit to open their blinkered minds wide to include all people from all nations.

Homogeneity cannot endure as God builds his Church.

And so we return to our original question: 'Which of these churches are we aiming to be?'

As inadequate as softmindedness is, a tough mind on its own, devoid of a tender heart, cannot represent Jesus faithfully. God is love, and: 'The hardhearted person never truly loves ... He is an isolated island. No outpouring of love links him with the mainland of humanity.'[22] To be hardhearted is to dehumanise and depersonalise. It's to give to charity but never of oneself. It's to critique without offering encouragement. It's to ignore the means in pursuit of the ends. It's to see people only for their usefulness – 'cogs in an ever-turning wheel'[23] – rather than for their innate worth. Serpents need doves.

For MLK, a significant part of faithful witness in the culture wars lies in non-violent resistance. It manages to avoid every pitfall, for it combines toughness and tenderness. It is how to 'oppose the unjust system and at the same time love the perpetrators of the system'.[24] This is the synthesised, third-way approach and the tough/tender motif lends itself well to speaking of God's own multi-faceted character and his action in the world: 'God has two outstretched arms. One is strong enough to surround us with justice, and one is gentle enough to embrace us with grace.'[25]

How can our church communities today embody strong justice and gentle grace in responding to the issues of our time? What does it look like to resist forces of evil non-violently, to be clear about what we stand for and why, while working out how to show love to those whose evil we are resisting?

Christmas every day

The birth of Jesus and the events surrounding it show that right from the beginning the gospel has been politically radical, subversive and revolutionary. Jesus was born to a poor, unmarried, unemployed, brown-skinned teenage mother who came from an area generally looked down on. He was born into a place and time in history where people were crying out for justice amid widespread political unrest. Very early in Jesus' life his family became political refugees when they fled a genocide. He wasn't born into a royal family. He was born Jewish in Palestine. It shouldn't be too hard to see, when we reflect on today's headlines, how very politically charged this entire scenario was.

Matthew's Gospel account records that at Jesus' birth there was a group of wise men looking for 'the one who has been born king' (2:2). We tend to gloss over this, but the specific language the wise men used would have been met with gasps, because in the Roman Empire no one is *born* a king, only *appointed* king by Caesar. But the wise men were adamant – they'd come looking for the one born as a king. Which means, here, 'king' is not so much a religious title as a political challenge to the systems of the day.

Mark too has specific language for Jesus, introducing him as 'Son of God' (1:1). This title was familiar at the time because it was reserved for Caesar alone. To call Jesus the Son of God was another challenge to the political power of the day. Jesus was the Christ – or Messiah. That title was understood by the Jews not religiously but politically, to mean 'the one who is liberator'. And so we can see that 'Jesus apparently set on transforming both the political and religious establishment by accepting the titles Son of David and Son of God.'[26] Are we really to believe that this liberating king has nothing to say about the weightiest issues of our time? Are we really to believe that prayers for revival don't include the rewiring of systems of the world? Should we honestly shun political debate as 'this-worldly' and so convey that our faith has nothing to say about how society functions? Is Jesus, this true Son of God, not that concerned by such things?

Prophetic imagination

When God says he is making all things new, what does this 'new' look like, and how can we get involved? That's the question that fuels prophetic imagination, and is my go-to thought process when I'm feeling a bit aimless: 'The task of prophetic ministry is to nurture, nourish, and evoke a consciousness and perception alternative to the consciousness and perception of the dominant culture around us.'[27]

When I seek to convey what the community of Manenberg is like I often have to think long and hard how I go about it. It's simply too easy to talk of the poverty, gangs, drugs and violence in isolation. While all of that does exist in Manenberg it's certainly not *all* that exists. Manenberg is full of life. Small children playing, teenagers choreographing dance routines to the latest Gqom release, old aunties stirring pots of breyani in animated conversation, taxi drivers leaning out of windows sharing jokes, young men walking the streets with huge bags of fruit or candyfloss to sell, people flocking to the sports field to cheer on their street's team in the local derby, played against the backdrop of the sun setting behind Table Mountain – this all exists *despite* the social ills.

Beyond the description of Manenberg as it currently is, I like to take time to dwell on the future potential for new realities that break cycles of dysfunction:

- The conversation with a gangster that ends with him explaining, through tears, how badly he wants to leave the gang. *Wouldn't it be amazing if he did?*
- The milestone of a recovering addict celebrating a year of sobriety, met by cheers from others on the same path. *Wouldn't it be cool if he stayed clean?*
- A young mother choosing to breathe slowly and take a walk rather than lash out as she navigates her healing from trauma. *Wouldn't it be wonderful if her child grew up in a safe environment?*

These examples and so many more point us to the prophetic potential all around us. The question is: 'Do we have eyes to see another city?'

Every city has a *shadow story* and a *prophetic promise*. The shadow story masquerades as normal, and the more it's reinforced by human belief and behaviour the more effectively it keeps the prophetic promise from coming forth. Culture wars are often fought based on shadow stories and, as such, tend to ignore the prophetic promise. If we believe only the shadow story we can get stuck in cynicism, blame and fear. But if we look for the prophetic promise we fuel imagination, wonder and creativity.

Shadow stories create fear and fear can create numbness. It's so easy to feel numb in the face of the sheer amount of need in the world. But as Walter Brueggemann explains, this numbness is both the expectation and result of unjust systems:

> Empires live by numbness. Empires … expect numbness about the human cost of war. Corporate economies expect

blindness to the cost in terms of poverty and exploitation. Governments and societies of domination go to great lengths to keep the numbness intact.[28]

If you feel a little numb with the state of the world, then one of the ways to learn to feel again is to use your imagination. What would it look like for my neighbourhood, or for that issue, to be transformed? Imagining prophetically works hand in hand with acting justly. As you begin to imagine a more just world, you'll find yourself inspired to live and act in ways that see it come about. And as you live and act in such ways, you'll begin to notice even more dreams developing in you for the kingdom coming on earth, which will in turn enthuse you to continue to live and act as a citizen of the kingdom of God. Thus is the world transformed as more and more people join in.

Pinch yourself. You are made up of matter in a world of physical things.

Matter matters.

We do not have some ethereal 'out there' hope – ours is rooted in dirt and soil, concrete and steel, forests and oceans, skyscrapers and rondavels, humans and nature. So a private, personal faith that has no recourse to actual physical things and lives is useless. It's worse than useless – it gives an illusion of hope but leaves things untouched by Jesus' good news worked out in his followers' hands, feet, ears and eyes put to worship.

Taking space seriously will include architecture that contributes to rather than undermines nature and aesthetics, sustainability and coherence; it will include rethinking urban landscapes that have maintained inequality and thus creating new possibilities for transformative encounters between people historically segregated from each other; it will include farming more sustainably (and (un) successfully), working the land as worship, not polluting it with short-term, high-yield pesticides in the name of profit. These are just examples of what the prophetic imagination could harness to collaborate with the Spirit to see God's will done on earth as in heaven.

A couple of passages I've found really helpful in thinking about prophetic promise are Isaiah 58 and 2 Chronicles 7:14. Both contain a familiar 'if … then' motif. In Chronicles, *if* God's people humble themselves, pray, seek his face, turn from wicked ways, *then* God will forgive their sin and heal their land. But this begs the rather obvious question: 'Which land *wouldn't* be healed by people humbling themselves, praying, seeking his face and turning from wicked ways?' The process is not transactional, like some tick-box exercise where God decides to heal some land as long as his people do certain things. The land is healed as a natural result of God's people changing their ways through turning their hearts to God.

The healing lies in the devoted lives and actions of God's people.

Similarly in Isaiah 58, God's people are told that true fasting is to loose the chains of injustice, untie cords of the yokes and then smash them and set the oppressed free. Sharing *our* food, sharing *our* homes and sharing *our* resources because we view the poor as *our* own flesh and blood – as family. Note that it doesn't say the *Church*'s food, home or resources – but *your* personal food, home and resources: this is defined as true worship.

Particularly in the West, where individualism has taken over our lives and faith, hospitality becomes something of a subversive resistance: your home is a temple, your table an altar, your food a sacrament. This needn't be a heavy burden – quite the opposite. *If* we do this, *then* we will discover something astonishing. As our lives are surrendered to God through the dismantling of injustice and through radical hospitality, we're told we will begin to notice changes in us:

> your light will break forth like the dawn, and your healing
> will quickly appear;
>   then your righteousness will go before you ...
> you will call, and the LORD will answer; you will cry for help,
> and he will say: here am I ...
> your night will become like the noonday.
> The LORD will guide you always; he will satisfy your needs in
> a sun-scorched land ... You will be like a well-watered garden,
> like a spring whose waters never fail.
> (Isaiah 58:8–11)

The promise is that God will go in front and behind of you, you will hear answers to your cries, hear the voice of God clearer, your needs will be satisfied, interior darkness will become light, your body will be strengthened and you'll be sustained like a well-watered garden.

Others can exhaust themselves waging culture wars, spreading fear, creating numbness. But being a faithful presence in society will refuse to engage on such terms. Isaiah tells us this defiance in the face of such division attracts God's faithful presence in our hearts.

Dismantling injustice is actually God's prescription for our own flourishing. But we have misunderstood life *after* death, which means we misunderstand the purpose of our life *before* death. Redefining the former has huge connotations for the latter.

You don't go to heaven, heaven comes to you

N. T. Wright suggests that "'God's kingdom" in the preaching of Jesus refers, not to post-mortem destiny, not to our escape from this world into another one, but to God's sovereign rule coming "on earth as it is in heaven".'[29] This is huge because:

> Heaven, in the Bible, is regularly not a future destiny, but the other, hidden dimension of our ordinary life – God's dimension if you like. God made heaven and earth; at the last, he will remake both, and join them together for ever.[30]

Which means:

> when we come to the picture of the actual End in Revelation 21 – 22, we find, not ransomed souls making their way to a disembodied heaven, but rather the new Jerusalem coming down from heaven to earth, uniting the two in a lasting embrace.[31]

This means Jesus didn't come to save us from earth but to empower us to renew the earth. Many – including many Christians – haven't understood the Christian view on resurrection after death. Because: 'As long as we see "Christian hope" in terms of "going to heaven", of a "salvation" which is essentially *away from* this world', there is no reason to think about what hope there is for 'change, rescue, transformation, new possibilities within the world in the present'.[32] The point is, if we're confused about our beyond-life hope we'll be confused about our on-earth mission.

The New Testament often uses the word 'saved' or 'salvation' to describe something quite physical. The bleeding woman who touched Jesus' clothes is told 'Your faith has saved you' (Luke 7:50).

And Matthew's account adds that 'the woman was saved from that moment on.'[33] Well hang on – yes, she received healing from sickness, but did she get *saved*? Well yes, she did – in the New Testament conception of the word: 'the New Testament often refers to "salvation" and "being saved" in terms of bodily events within the present world'[34] and not just life after death. It conceives of salvation as the inbreaking of the kingdom of God into the structures and pain of this world. This means salvation can't only be applied individualistically. You're saved for the purposes of what God now longs to do through your life. Beyond the personal experience of forgiveness, joy and peace that salvation in Jesus brings, it's also designed to be used in public, for the benefit of others. Your life is a foretaste for those around you of what the kingdom is really like. Your life is a 'try before you buy' sample for everyone around you: 'What's more [we] are not just to be a sign and foretaste of that ultimate "salvation"; [we] are to be *part of the means by which* God makes this happen in both the present and in the future.'[35] Could this be what Paul means when he says the world is groaning for the sons and daughters of God to be revealed?

There is an eventual state to which creation is currently heading, where God's will is really done on earth as it is in heaven. That is the goal to which all life, indeed the whole of creation, is orientated. Our work is to co-labour with this vision here and now – which is a much richer work than simply trying to get people to sign up to heaven when they die or put God to one side and get our heads down in striving towards earthly justice in our own efforts.

Hands and feet

Jesus told us to pray to the Father: 'your will be done, on earth as in heaven' (Matthew 6:10). And he replies: 'I am making everything new!' (Revelation 21:5). His chosen way of making things new, of pervading earth with heaven, of bringing forth his rule and reign, is (drumroll please):

You and me!

Us.

The Church (eek).

We are to prepare the way of the Lord. That isn't grandiose or triumphalist, it is our God-given mandate. There are countless issues to address in the world and we can't all do everything – but is there any more compelling argument for being (un)successful than that the things we're striving for are killing us? Here are four biggies I'm convinced followers of Jesus need to engage with in our quest for (un)success:

Financial inequality and poverty fuelled by greed and globalisation

COVID exposed and exacerbated many concerning global trends, one of which was the sharply growing gap between rich and poor. If it's true that 'a successful society is a progress machine [that] takes in the raw material of innovations and produces broad human advancement', then it should be no surprise that as the world grows increasingly unequal, 'There is a spreading recognition on both sides of the ideological divide, that the system is broken and has to change.'[36]

Racial oppression fuelled by historic injustice

Imagine you're playing in a soccer match. Your team has eleven players but the opposition has twenty. Your team isn't allowed to make substitutions but the opposition is. The goal you are to score in is half the size of the goal you're defending. And to top it off, the pitch is on a slope so you're playing uphill. You've been playing for 500 years and are now losing 1,000 to zero. Someone comes along and points out to the opposition that this is unfair. So the various inequalities are corrected and the pitch is levelled. You continue to play but the opposition can't understand why you still have an issue with the conditions. 'Stop complaining. We've made it equal now!' they say, ignoring the fact that they're winning by 1,000 goals, each of which was scored in grossly unfair conditions. You continue to protest but are now labelled 'angry', 'entitled' or 'divisive', and your advocacy for a pitch slanting the other way for the next 500 years to truly even out the match conditions falls on deaf ears.

We need to do an honest examination of the world we live in and wake up to the fact that for many of us in the West, so many of our present-day societies have been formed not by Christian ideals but by principles formed by a colonial moral ecology. This isn't 'cultural Marxism', it's just blindingly obvious. The sheer fact of language assigning positive value to whiteness and negative value to blackness points to this. For example: to be blacklisted is to be deemed undesirable either economically or morally; a white lie is deemed less bad than a 'regular' lie; blackmail is illegal; at weddings brides wear white dresses; at funerals mourners wear black; the Dark Ages marked a period of intellectual decline vs the Enlightenment, a period of philosophical creativity.

War and violence fuelled by nationalism and corporate profit

'Christian nationalism' might be as much of an oxymoron as 'Microsoft Works', 'Jumbo shrimp' or 'Christian self-help'.[37] The irony of militarised foreign policy is that it 'proliferates death in the name of a life that would be free from it'.[38] Jesus was neither nationalistic nor violent and yet today, in the West especially, Christians are known for being both. Whereas Jesus preached fidelity to God alone, laying down our lives for our friends alongside praying for our enemies, the absurdity of nationalism is that it encourages an idolatrous relationship to the nation state akin to 'being asked to die for the telephone company'.[39]

Environmental destruction fuelled by consumerism and economic growth

When considering the connection between unfettered economic growth as a sign of a successful administration, alongside the simultaneous destruction of our natural environment, we'd do well to remember words of the writer and activist Edward Abbey: 'Growth for the sake of growth *is* the ideology of the cancer cell.'[40]

These are, of course, massive issues. But one way that (un)successful followers of Jesus can show our faithful presence is through speaking into these and many other framing issues in our time. And whether we like it or not, we can't do this without engaging with politics.

The great levelling

You may have heard of something called the Seven Mountains Mandate. In short, it's a teaching that says Christians are to 'invade and occupy' the world's systems to usher in the end times. And so, the teaching goes, we must seek influence and power to transform society in seven different spheres: media, government, education, economy, religion, family and the arts. That is what successful Christians do. Apparently.

Not sure what you think? Fair enough. It's had its fair share of critics.

I imagine the prophet Isaiah may have been one such critic (despite the fact that Isaiah 2:2 is used as a key verse in the Seven Mountains

Mandate!). Have a look at how Isaiah says the coming of the Lord will take place:

> In the wilderness prepare the way for the LORD; make straight in the desert a highway for our God. *Every valley shall be raised up, every mountain and hill made low*; the rough ground shall become level, the rugged places a plain. And the glory of the LORD will be revealed, and all people will see it together. (40:3–5)

In preparing the coming of God, valleys are to be raised up and mountains made low. Doing this will result in the glory of the Lord being revealed and all humankind seeing it, unable to deny it. Isaiah is clear – the coming of the Lord will be marked by valleys being raised up, not by Christians trying to climb mountains. This is the irony: in trying to bring Jesus into the world's systems to 'purify' them, Christians often end up doing the opposite: bringing the world's value systems into our faith in Jesus, resulting in a weird triumphalism.

It is the epitome of conceit to pursue power and influence in order to have a platform to exhibit the humility and servanthood of Jesus.

So what's the answer? If we shouldn't seek to gain power to respond to systemic injustice, what *should* we do? If we shouldn't seek to gain profile and power on the world's terms to usher in a new era of Christian dominance, what *should* we do?

We should give our lives to the raising up of the valleys.

Or as Vinoth Ramachandra, a theologian with a PhD in nuclear engineering, so explicitly puts it:

there can be no conversion to Christ that does not entail, at the same time, a conversion towards the men, women and children at the bottom of our societies who bear the costs of the peace, wealth and security enjoyed by the few at the top.[41]

What might the seven valleys of society be? Well, my friend Bob came up with a list that I think is pretty spot on. He suggests the seven valleys could be: prisons, slums, old people's homes, psychiatric wards, drug dens, refugee camps and those without houses. In short, the seven valleys are places in which a lot of Jesus' followers are already active. The Church is well known across the world for being a servant in the valleys – making the rough places just a little smoother. But there's so much more for us to imagine.

Can you imagine what might happen if the Church put as much strategy and ambition into infiltrating the seven valleys of society as it does into trying to climb the seven mountains of influence? Can you imagine how much more prophetic authority and influence we would have in society, due to lives laid down rather than trying to grab power? Can you imagine the delight of God as his followers put first those the world puts last? Can you imagine those previously far from God, kneeling in incredulity and wonder as 'the glory of the Lord is revealed' and they witness the Church being what it was always meant to be? Can you imagine our influence in all spheres of society if we were to forsake any vestige of earthly success in our quest to go ever lower in our worship of Jesus the penniless Messiah?

Can you imagine the stinging words of the culture wars quietening as the faithful actions of (un)successful Jesus followers quietly transform culture?

Questions for reflection

1 What do you think about some of the claims of this chapter – for example, that the gospel is inherently political, that heaven isn't a destination we go to, that Christians are called to engage with culture? What are the connotations for your life?

2 Why does it matter we see Jesus as liberator from unjust systems as well as personal saviour?

3 What is a kingdom moral economy? Do you have prophetic imagination for what your part in it could be?

4 How do you think the Church could represent Jesus more faithfully in today's culture wars?

5 Have you heard of the Seven Mountains Mandate? Do you agree it is problematic? Why might it be more popular than a seven-valleys faith? What are the consequences of our ignoring the valleys?

6

Success is ... Living in power and participation

On suffering and the supernatural

What's amazing to me about a man like you
Is that you raised the dead but had to suffer too, Jesus.
(Jason Upton[1])

To have a theology of suffering without a theology of power is
to pervert the gospels.
(Rob Reimer[2])

Co-suffering love is the only power, force or strength that
anyone can ever have for the healing of another human soul.
(Vladika Lazar Puhalo[3])

It's been said that what comes to mind when you think about God
is the most important thing about you.[4] How does that make you
feel? Are you comforted or made anxious by what your relationship
to God says about you?

We've seen how the culture wars of the day have too often witnessed
the Church divide rather than unite on how it seeks to represent
Jesus successfully to our increasingly polarised world. Sadly, this
brittle mindset of this-or-that, black-and-white thinking isn't just
undermining how the Church chooses to relate to the world, it's
impacting how we relate to God ourselves. Culture wars seem to go
right to the heart of our experience *of* God and *with* God.

While the culture wars prey on some of our deepest fears – of public shaming, humiliation, being wrong or guilty, being misunderstood, feeling we don't belong – our relationship with God should be our safest place, where our fears are put to rest and we find our ultimate place of belonging. But the problem with fear is that it seeks control. As the fears of prevailing culture seep into our friendship with God, we seek to control aspects of our faith. And though control is an effective short-term antidote to fear because it meets our need of immediate – but counterfeit – certainty, it will ultimately render us unable to yield to God's leading and unwilling to discover new facets of his character, leaving us vulnerable to being carried by the currents of culture.

Our fear of falling for fake news will lead to a fear of falling for false theological teaching. Our echo chamber of news outlets will be matched only by the narrow voices we listen to in regard to our faith. And in our desire to be viewed positively by those we relate to, we wouldn't dare entertain any perspectives that rock our tribe's theological boat. Our loyalty to one perspective at the expense of all others dismembers the body of Christ.

Sigh.

As basic as this is, here is where we must begin.

It's just so easy to align ourselves with one perspective to the exclusion of all others, however subconsciously. But let's not confuse control with wisdom or narrow-mindedness with discernment. You can be a fan of K-Pop *and* Country; support Tottenham Hotspur and *not* hate Arsenal. Deliberately frivolous examples, but if we're able to view *any* polarising issue a little differently, where we aren't just forced to take one side or the other, there might emerge creative potential for new paradigms of thought and praxis.

This could have some really positive connotations for how we relate to God.

An area in which this black-and-white, this-or-that thinking has led to dangerous polarisation in the Church is our approach to the supernatural and the natural; raw passion and com-passion; what we might now call Revivalism and Activism. Though the Apostle Paul highlights these as two keys for what it means to know Christ – 'I want to know Christ – yes, to know the power of his resurrection and participation in his sufferings' (Philippians 3:10) – we have too often split the two. We've tended to ignore Holy Spirit power in our participation with those who are suffering, rendering us powerless to bring deliverance for the afflicted and unable to persevere in difficult or distressing environments. Or we've pursued supernatural power within our church meetings (but often for our own ends), and failed to translate this into bringing hope to the plight of the most vulnerable or into the systems of the world that perpetuate such pain.

I believe we desperately need both the compassion of God combined with the power of God to (un)successfully transform communities and cities. We'll end up blowing up on power alone and burning out on compassion alone:

> Justice and supernatural power are connected … Works of mercy and works of power belong together. We are the people of miracles and mercy. Those of us who love miracles are being called to love mercy too. Those of us who love mercy are called to walk in the miraculous. It's the Jesus way.[5]

In a world that loves to pick a side you may well find yourself accused of being too 'participatory suffering' by some and not enough 'resurrection power' by others. Yet I believe the (un)successful follower of

Jesus will have to come to terms with being both too much and not enough for either side of the theological spectrum. We need to be prepared to stick our head above the parapet of tribal loyalty across different expressions of church, because 'living without compassion isn't an option. Neither is going without power.'[6]

Personally I'm so convinced of the importance of bringing together these two perspectives that it's something I'm willing to give the rest of my life to living out.

If this chapter does what I intend it to, maybe you will too.

Jumping in

We have an annual retreat for our Tree of Life core leadership team at the beginning of each year, when we reflect on the previous twelve months and do our best to plot a course through the coming year; the retreat weekends are a time for deep soul-connection and are usually a highlight of our year. One year, however, we were getting nowhere.

There was a shared acknowledgement that various issues had emerged between us but been ignored. Until we addressed these we knew we couldn't find agreement on events we were reflecting on from the previous year, let alone envision the coming one. It was also the first time Sarah and I had participated in one of these weekends as parents, and Simi was fifteen months old at the time, loud and energetic, needing constant attention and grabbing anything within reach of her adorable, chubby little fingers.

By the final day I was exhausted and crabby, so when the facilitator posed the question to the group 'What are you trusting God for in this next year?' I ignored the invitation and instead went off on a rant about how suffocated I was feeling with the seemingly endless cycle of issues and needs in our church community. With a jaded sigh I looked up at the ceiling and asked no one in particular 'Why won't God just do something supernatural?' I'd managed to kill the vibe completely, and the first session of the morning finished on a low as we went through to the kitchen to make breakfast. While I was frying some eggs, Leon came into the kitchen looking subdued. He'd just been to check up on Cynthy, his wife, who was pregnant and had missed the session because she was in so much pain from sciatica nerve compression running from her lower back down her legs. It had been a constant problem for her over the last six years but would particularly flare up during pregnancy. She was lying in the bath, in great pain and hardly able to move, let alone take part in the sessions. We began to discuss whether the best thing might be for them to pack up and leave early so she could go and see a doctor. As we stared into space unsure what to do, a lingering silence settled in the room. Then Clare suddenly piped up: 'Guys can't we at least go and pray for Cynth? If she has to leave early then fine, but let's make sure we've covered her in prayer first.'

Confession: I was only half committed to the conversation.

To my shame, I hadn't emerged the other side of my negative rant and prioritised my appetite for breakfast over my friend's very real need for healing. I was *hangry* – frustrated with how little I felt we'd accomplished over the weekend and just wanting to eat and get going on the next session. I suppose I thought we'd already had so many discussions on how best to help Cynth with her pain; we'd prayed on multiple occasions and seen nothing change (I know – I can be a real idiot). And besides, I'd waited patiently in line to use the stove, my eggs were now almost done and the toast was about to pop up. So I made up my mind – I wasn't going to participate in praying for Cynth, I was going to eat my breakfast.

About ten minutes later, as I was putting my plate in the dish-washer, screams started coming from Cynthy's room on the other side of the house. I stifled an eggy burp and looked out of the large glass sliding door into the garden.

What – on – earth?

It was raining and cold outside and the wind was blowing hard, but there was Cynthy running across the grass barefoot, jumping up and down and shouting. Her face was covered in the widest smile I've ever seen. I felt like one of those cartoon characters with eyes popping out on stalks and jaw hitting the ground as they witness something mind-blowing. I ran outside, narrowly avoiding bumping into Clare, who was quietly sobbing as she stood watching Cynth. And then Clare looked at me. She didn't need to say anything. I immediately felt pangs of conviction.

'Supernatural enough for you?' she asked, grinning through tears. I had no words.

Leon ambled over and joined Cynthy on the grass and gave her one of his big bear hugs. She folded into his arms and just began weeping uncontrollably. Years of pain and disappointment, count-less doctor's visits and bills, whole periods of life being physically carried to the bathroom, unable to run for six years – all of it flooded out in that moment in those tears in that embrace.

Later on, when we'd all calmed down a bit, I asked Cynth what had happened:

> Well, when I last gave birth my hip went out of place and has never realigned. This caused a discrepancy in my legs, and my right leg was about three centimetres shorter. And

that meant a whole lot of pain and decreased movement. To make things worse, sciatica pain has been flaring up in this pregnancy as the baby grows. So this morning I was lying in bed and realised I couldn't get up, let alone walk, so I sat in bed feeling sorry for myself. But then Clare and Zi burst into my room and said they were going to pray for this to end. As they prayed, the pain in my left leg stopped. And then the craziest thing happened. I felt a sensation moving down my leg and the pain left. I asked Clare if she'd seen anything happen and she said she had felt the leg move but hadn't wanted to say anything! So I put my legs out straight, and they were now exactly the same length! I touched my hip, and the usual protrusion was no longer there either. I had to test this out and as I got to my feet the pain was completely gone. I walked around in disbelief and just began to sob because this was the first pain-free walking I'd done in years. It was raining outside but I didn't care. I just wanted to run around free from pain.

Jesus has power to heal all sickness and invites his followers to wield this power lovingly on his behalf. Clare and Zi had believed in this power enough to do something about Cynthy's pain, but there could have been two opposite and equally problematic approaches to trying to help Cynthy's condition had they not known how to hold the tension between this holy power and participation so well. On the one hand, you could ignore the pain Cynth was in and march her around the garden shouting out Bible verses on healing to 'claim her miracle'. I've seen this sort of thing play out and it can create deep shame and resentment if nothing happens. On the other hand, it would be equally wrong to sit next to her with a box of tissues lamenting her pain but failing to invite the supernatural power of God to heal her. I've seen this happen too, and it can create a resigned self-pity.

While I knew deep down that Cynthy needed both power and participation, I lacked either. Witnessing years of no breakthrough in Cynthy's condition led me to do all the wrong things – I'd hardened my heart to Clare's suggestion that morning, refused to engage with Cynthy's suffering and traded empathy for eggs on toast. I'd given up on God's power to heal and so I gave up entering into fellowship with Cynthy in her suffering.

Wet coal

'Loadshedding' might not be a term you've come across but if you live in South Africa you'll know precisely what it means. Loadshedding is where Eskom, the state electricity provider, cuts supply to certain neighbourhoods at scheduled times to take the strain off the grid (at which point you spend the next five minutes stumbling around in the dark looking for candles). Many believe it's a hangover from the Zuma presidency, when public funds were regularly ransacked by government ministers. Either way it's a huge inconvenience, meaning hospitals, schools and other much-needed services have to plan for outages on a regular basis. In fact it's estimated that the South African economy could be 10% larger without loadshedding,[7] which costs businesses across the country up to 900 million Rand (*c*.£38 million) a day due to having to close or being disrupted.[8] When asked why it's so difficult to generate electricity (kind of the main purpose of an electricity company), various Eskom spokespersons have on more than one occasion made the excuse that *the coal was wet*. Yes, you read that right. A huge state-owned enterprise, employing over 44,000 people, is unable to keep coal from getting wet.[9]

In many ways I feel this is a parable for my life. Maybe it rings true for you too?

Might we also experience a lack of power more often than we'd like because we fail to keep our coal dry? Lack of devotion and discipline in our private, unseen habits and behaviours can so often undermine our public life and ministry. I'm not even talking about huge scandals or what we euphemistically call 'moral failures' (Christian code for things like having affairs or embezzling money), just a diffident half-heartedness in how we steward the health of our soul.

At various points in my own journey I've wondered whether it would be easier to keep my 'coal dry' in another environment. At times it's even led me to judge someone else's suffering unfairly. I remember once sitting next to a pastor at a large dinner event in the UK. We'd met a couple of times before but he introduced himself again and proceeded to tell me all about his ministry (I kept my thoughts below to myself):

My church is in one of the most deprived boroughs in London. Our foodbank is so busy we can hardly keep up, but thankfully people are donating much more food now – it makes you think about the level of poverty in the UK and that the government really isn't doing enough.

(What, you have a thriving, well-coordinated, fully-stocked, volunteer-led initiative, operating out of churches all around the country so the hungry get fed? How wonderful!)

Our borough is also the worst for knife crime in the whole city. You should see how many knives get deposited in the knife amnesty bin, it's shocking.

(So you have bins where large numbers of people surrender their weapons voluntarily, without police intervention? And nobody breaks into these bins and steals all the knives? Amazing!)

Returning to Cape Town the following day I was met with a message from a friend asking for money to buy food. As I waited for my luggage to arrive I passed a newspaper headline that caught my eye: 'Two Policemen Shot Dead for their Guns'. And I thought of the conversations I'd shared the night before, perhaps unfairly wondering how much easier it would be to see power break out in *his* environment or even to participate in *his* suffering. And yet God soon reminded me of some foundational truths that can be all too easy to forget.

God can make life grow anywhere and in any conditions, and if he's called you to a place and a people, your responsibility is simply to sow yourself there, wholeheartedly. Then as you struggle and strain and have faith for the unseen (Hebrews 11:1), as you grow muscle strength removing stones (Isaiah 62:10) to help create an environment conducive to growth, as you give yourself fully to the work you've been called to do (1 Corinthians 15:58), you'll begin to see *yourself* changing.

Although as a human with free will there's no guarantee of what you'll change into. You'll either become hardened or softened – it's your choice. The psychiatrist Elisabeth Kübler-Ross, a great expert on death and dying, reminds us that there's always the possibility of beauty the other side of suffering:

The most beautiful people we have known are those who have known defeat, known suffering, known struggle, known loss, and have found their way out of the depths. These people have an appreciation, a sensitivity, and an understanding of life that fills them with compassion, gentleness, and a deep loving concern. Beautiful people do not just happen.[10]

You can live wherever you feel you are called. You can do life among whomever God has given you a particular affinity for. You are free to live life however you best imagine fits what you know of Jesus. The difference in living sacrificially rather than cheaply, whether in London, Manenberg or anywhere else, boils down to one word: death.

(Un)success = death.

Gulp.

Lay it down

A favourite passage of mine is found in John chapter 10, where Jesus refers to himself as the good shepherd. It tends to be popular for the tweetable soundbite in verse 10: 'I have come that they may have life, and have it to the full.' We shout a hearty 'Amen' when we hear that one. It feels good to know that Jesus offers us abundant life – there's absolutely nothing wrong with that. And I believe that he does because, despite my perennial hang-ups and insecurities, I experience this fullness of life regularly. Perhaps you do too?

So what does this look like and how do we successfully access this fullness of life Jesus seems to be offering? This verse can come across – and I've heard it used as such – like a marketing slogan, dangling a golden carrot in front of sad or vulnerable people to recruit them into church.

Well, we need to read on to grasp its whole meaning. Jesus explains what the good shepherd does: he 'lays down his life for the sheep' (v. 11). If we keep reading we see this refrain again and again: 'I lay down my life for the sheep' (v. 15); 'The reason my Father loves me is that I lay down my life' (v. 17).

Jesus' point is that fullness of life is found in laying down our lives. You cannot find true abundance any other way. This directly relates to Philippians 3, where we're told that 'becoming like him in his death' leads to 'attaining to the resurrection from the dead' (vv. 10, 11). The paradox of kingdom success is that it is hidden in the most unsuccessful-looking things: laying down your life leads to fullness; becoming like Jesus in his death leads to resurrection; participation in the example of Jesus' suffering leads to power: 'For success, like happiness, cannot be pursued; it must ensue, and it only does so as the unintended side-effect of one's surrender to a person other than oneself.'[11]

Like a lot of what Jesus said, this all sounds a little disconcerting to modern ears. We're all meant to become nuns or something? Or if we don't get killed for our faith then we're sell-outs. Or at the very least, God is trying to find ways to wrestle the things we love out of our hands so we can serve his will without any distraction from fun or enjoyment.

Well no, not exactly.

And as if to pre-empt such wonky radicalising, Jesus restates: 'I lay down my life – only to take it up again. No one takes it from me, but I lay it down of my own accord' (John 10:17–18).

Like Jesus, each of us has free will to lay down our life:

> If you've known the love of God, if you've tasted of his sweet-ness at all, there's no other way to serve him except giving up your life. And this is voluntary. This is not the sentence of death at all. We're not sentenced to death, we're just privileged to answer his call.[12]

You might be thinking: 'Well hang on a minute, Jesus died for the sins of humanity – we can't all do that!' Absolutely right, and please don't try. But in dying and raising to life again, Jesus foreshadowed the journey of surrender and rebirth that each person who chooses to follow him must go through. He reiterated this when he said: 'unless a grain of wheat falls into the earth and dies, it remains alone; but if it dies, it bears much fruit' (John 12:24 RSV). As C. S. Lewis said: 'Nothing that you have not given away will be really yours. Nothing in you that has not died will ever be raised from the dead.'[13] When we put our faith in him we each willingly give up our life as we know it – we lay it down – so that we can take up our new life in him. This new life of following Jesus – where we seek to align our desires, loves and motivations, our use of time and energy, words and actions with his – comes to resemble the promise of life in its fullness.

Remember: your most compelling answer to the question 'What is success?' isn't communicable by words, only by your very life.

Digging deeper

In our pursuit of the kind of success Jesus desires we can draw out from Philippians 3:10 some practical ways to live that help us 'lay down' our lives.

'I want to know Christ': contemplation

Where we go for our peace, our purpose and our healing will define how we show up in the world. There's a huge difference between social justice fuelled by an ideology and kingdom justice fuelled by the Spirit. Our starting – and ending – place is knowing the presence and love of Jesus. Always. We never graduate beyond that. Which means that prayer in all its forms – intercession, contemplation, silence, thankfulness, testimony or whatever – really is everything (see Figure 1).

> I want to know Christ and the power of his resurrection, and the fellowship of sharing in his sufferings, becoming like him in his death ...

PRAYER SOLITUDE SILENCE FASTING

Figure 1 **The foundation of how we show up in the world –
contemplating Jesus**

I'm glad the charismatic church seems to be coming round to the inadequacy of a theology that screams ever louder the mantra 'Your breakthrough is coming!' but leaves people damaged and despairing when it doesn't. I believe this is what has drawn younger generations into a rediscovery of the spiritual disciplines, as a way of rooting ourselves in inner satisfaction and recognition of God.

The great theologian Thomas Merton said: 'Our real journey in life is interior: it is a matter of growth, deepening, and of an ever greater surrender to the creative action of love and grace in our hearts.'[14] Everything you do and the effect you have on your world flows from God's activity within you. But while I fully subscribe to the importance of a rule of life that orientates our longings around Jesus, I sometimes get nervous that the current emphasis on spiritual disciplines can be un-self-aware-ingly white and privileged. For example: you need to have a phone or computer with internet connection in the first place to have a 'digital sabbath'; solitude isn't much of an option for those living in self-made shacks in informal settlements; people without food have to fast whether they like it or not. Then there's simplicity as a spiritual discipline. Friends of mine who are incredibly intentional about living simply once told me of a camping holiday they went on with friends who'd grown up in a township. The campsite's only running water was from the nearby stream and there was no electricity. All very basic, low-carbon-footprinty and technologically-detoxy. A couple of days into the holiday my friends asked their companions how they were enjoying their first camping experience:

> Yeah, it's all right, but we just can't see what the attraction is for white people in going on holiday and playing 'township township'. We grew up with no running water and electricity, so we find this 'simplicity' thing just reminds us of a life we thought we'd left behind.

Our spiritual disciplines root us in the goodness of God but they're also grounded in our geographical and economic realities. It's important that we check our blind spots before preaching a particular 'rule' or rhythm of life. It's also important that our motivation is not to be 'in' with the millennial in-crowd but to be enfolded further and further within the love of God. He has made us all to be so beautifully unique and I think it's therefore likely that our particular pattern for abiding in him will reflect who we are. If spiritual disciplines truly change us internally then they'll always turn our perspective outward – to living with and caring for the most vulnerable around us.

'The power of his resurrection': revivalism

As we abide in God's presence, connected to the vine (as Jesus put it in John 15), we find we become increasingly aware of heaven's perspective and we begin to align our limited imaginations with God's unlimited power, and that sparks faith for the impossible (see Figure 2).

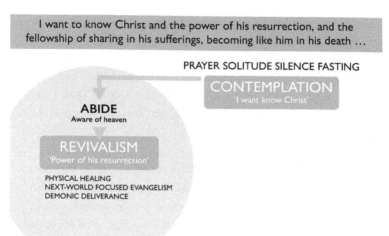

Figure 2 **Abiding in heaven's perspective fuels faith for the miraculous**

And with this faith comes a desire to do what Jesus did, as in Acts 10:38: 'God anointed Jesus of Nazareth with the Holy Spirit and power, and ... he went around *doing good* and *healing* all who were under the power of the devil, because *God was with him*.' Sharing our faith through evangelism, deliverance and healing, done in the power of God, isn't fringe 'charismania', it's conventional Christianity and there is a *purpose* to it all:

Christ's presence in us is 'the hope of glory' (Colossians 1:27).

His presence is his Holy Spirit.

The Holy Spirit enables us to address people's problems super-naturally, with a power way beyond our own as we play our part in transforming society.

'Participation in his sufferings': activism

Spending time contemplating Christ – getting to *know* him better – can lead us towards abiding in heaven's culture on the one hand but also lamenting our world's culture on the other (see Figure 3).

'But wait a minute Pete,' I hear you say, 'you said (un)success is about bringing together both power and participation – and now you're splitting the two into different sides of a flow chart.' I hear you. It does look a bit like that, but we need to be able to hold these two seemingly contrasting perspectives in one breath. One person who appeared to grasp this well was Helen H. Lemmel, the woman who wrote the classic hymn 'Turn your eyes upon Jesus'. Though the words to the now-famous chorus speak of our focus on the world dimming as we gaze at Christ's wonderful face, the perhaps lesser-known third verse goes on to encourage believers to turn outwards to the dying world around them and share of Jesus' perfect salvation and will for the world. Heaven's culture changes earth's culture.

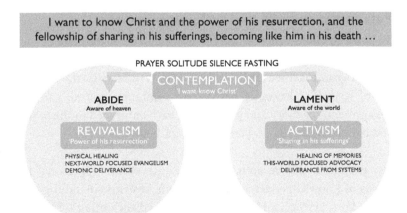

Figure 3 **Lamenting the pain of the world leads to faithful action**

As we wrestle with the challenge of Scripture we're jolted out of our warm fuzzies and compelled to go out into a dying world. In and out. Breathe in the refreshing of God's presence and breathe out his glory and grace into the world. In this way the flipside of abiding in God's presence is lamenting for our world as it is. As you pray for the world you become aware of the pain all around us. It doesn't take much more than a cursory glance over the day's news headlines to recognise we live in a mess – wars and environmental disasters, paedophilia and racial oppression, suicide and political corruption. Whatever it is that grabs your attention and moves your spirit to intercede and then do something, activism flowing from contemplation needs to be fuelled by hope. That doesn't mean we shouldn't get angry about things. Hope and anger are not opposed to each other, as a quote often attributed to St Augustine reminds us: 'Hope has two beautiful daughters; their names are Anger and Courage. Anger at the way things are, and Courage to see that they do not remain as they are.'

A righteous anger gives us the courage to engage with unjust systems of the world and bring hope in place of despair.

Personal prophetic and systemic prophetic

To abide in God's other-worldly power and lament the state of the world around us – inhaling and exhaling – is to bring revivalism and activism together. This is what N. T. Wright calls 'the double life of Jesus'.[15] A heavenly perspective combines with an earthly engagement, the glory and grit of faith, each enmeshed in the other and connected by the prophetic (see Figure 4).

The prophetic can be both personal and systemic – personal in words of knowledge, destiny and wisdom, systemic in calling out unjust laws, systems and practices. Both need each other – badly – and hold the two sides of our 'breathing-in-and-out' faith together in harmony.

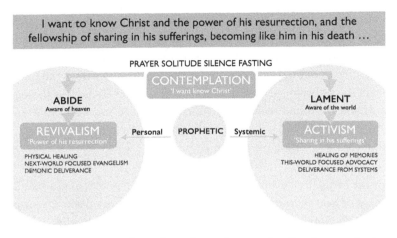

Figure 4 **Heaven and earth are brought together by the prophetic**

Bringing it together

I was kneeling at the front of hundreds of people, eyes closed, responding to an altar call at a Christian gathering. As music played from the stage I could hear the hushed tones of others around me praying for each other. Someone came up to me and put a hand on my shoulder. Whispering into my ear just loud enough to hear, he gave me a couple of prophetic words he felt were from God. I nodded, eyes closed, smiling, sensing resonance with what he said. Then after a brief pause, and with slightly less confidence in his voice, he said something that caught me off-guard:

> I wouldn't usually say this. If it makes no sense, then feel free to disregard it. It's just that I have another word for you. I feel like God is saying 'Now is the time to become a father – now is the time to adopt.'

I opened my eyes in a flash and looked at him, incredulous. It wasn't so much that he would give such a punchy prophetic word – granted it was a risky one – but that he'd said almost exactly the same thing as someone else a couple of hours earlier in the pub across the road from the gathering venue. That afternoon another friend had shared a dream she'd had recently, in which she'd seen me with children around me and had a clear sense the dream related to adoption, and that God was telling me the time was now.

In the venue that evening, as I sat on the floor processing, I had a sense of heaven touching earth – God's will and my desire coming together. I knew it was right. Before we'd even met each other, Sarah and I had both wanted to adopt children. We hadn't been clear on the timing but now it seemed there was an invitation to get the ball rolling.

We enquired with Child Welfare and began filling out the forms and praying for the social worker who would be assigned to us. In response to our lament at how the world was, we'd orientated our lives around young men in pain from addiction and gangs and were now choosing to bring an orphaned child into our family. We prayed that our life choices – specifically sharing our home with those some would deem dangerous – wouldn't count against us in the adoption application, and that our social worker would either share, or at least be sympathetic to, our faith. A month or so later we were sitting next to each other looking at the two social workers in front of us, thumbing through our application form.

'You say it's been a tough last year, would you care to elaborate?'
'Yup, sure. I mean, it's a long story but basically just over a year ago one of the young men living with us was killed in a car

crash. It was completely out of the blue, and we'd been like parent figures to him as he'd come to live with us to get free from drugs and gangs.'

The social worker nodded and frowned. Then suddenly both her eyebrows shot up and she fixed her now wide-open eyes on us: 'What was the young man's name?' she asked.

'Maruwaan.'

Her jaw hit the floor, her eyes began to tear up and she replied, in a near whisper, 'He lived with *you*?'

'Yes, but why, did ... did you know him?!'

'No, but I saw a film about his life on TV. And when I watched it, I just wept. It was so beautiful.'

'We made that film! Wow! So ... ummm ... are you saying the guys we live with won't jeopardise our adoption process?'

'Not at all! When I was watching Maruwaan's film, I kept thinking "If only more places like that existed for people struggling with addiction."'

When Sarah and I got into our car at the end of the interview we couldn't stop beaming. God had gone before us. We sensed we were walking in what felt like the slipstream of God's favour. I was convinced we would be parents in a matter of weeks after that meeting. We redecorated our spare room, bought all the baby paraphernalia and told everyone who would listen that we could be parents 'anytime now'.

For months and months, every time either of our phones rang our hearts skipped a beat and we looked at each other, eyebrows raised and fingers crossed. But despite the remarkable prophetic words and our social worker having been floored by Maruwaan's story, every complication and bureaucratic delay that could have happened did happen.

Eventually, after two years of waiting, we began to lose hope. A settled sadness, like a raincloud over my head, followed me around. We moved the cot out of the spare room and put a bed in there instead. We folded up the baby clothes and packed them away. It was just really confusing. We'd seen God initiate our adoption process through confirmation of powerful prophecy and unprecedented favour with Child Welfare. He'd even provided miraculously for the adoption fees (money that we didn't have). We'd prayed and mobilised others to pray. We'd fasted and contended, abiding in God's promises, reminding ourselves of the miracles that had got us to this point. We were trying to match our personal prophetic words with a systemic prophetic approach to parenting, and studied trans-racial adoption and the need for healing of memories in adopted children. We'd advocated for the importance of adoption where no other option exists, with those unconvinced by our choices. We'd chosen godparents who could assist our child in finding their place in the world. And yet here we were, feeling the dejection of prayer unanswered and hope deferred. It just felt as though God had lost the enthusiasm he'd shown at first or had moved on and had better things to do – or something. The wait from registering to adopt to finally becoming parents was three and a half years. That's a pretty long pregnancy. But of course, when we were eventually matched with our daughter and she came home, all the pain of such a long wait dissipated in new-parent joy. We called her Simthandile, meaning 'beloved'.

When it comes to our beloved daughter we can look back with hindsight and safely say that the wrestle of holding resurrection power and participatory suffering in constant tension for all those years was worth it. And yet there have been other situations that spring to mind where the wait is still ongoing and the miracle we're waiting for still hasn't come – I imagine you can think of some too. One situation that will always remain with me is of a young man we knew and loved called Roscoe.

Roscoe was in a bit of a pickle, having been caught by police in possession of a semi-automatic weapon. As he was also a member of a gang it was fairly obvious he wasn't planning on using this gun for a weekend of clay-pigeon shooting or big-game hunting. He was looking at an eight-year sentence. So we wrote letters, met with a lawyer and appealed to the magistrate to allow him to live with us. We knew it was highly unlikely but we prayed and left it in God's hands. It genuinely felt like a miracle when the magistrate redirected him our way, stipulating that he had to live with us for the eighteen-month duration of our residential programme and that if he left, we were to inform the court, who would then take him to prison. Sometime later, and with Roscoe confessing to having thoughts of committing acts of serious violence towards members of our group, a psychiatrist confirmed Roscoe had a personality disorder, exhibited sociopathic tendencies, and that it was not safe for him to be with us. He had to go, but where? To jail for the next eight years? To a mental hospital? Were those the only options? And what of God's miracle-working power that, we were convinced, had brought Roscoe to us in the first place – couldn't God heal him? We'd prayed through his traumatic past, about his violent present and for his future, but nothing seemed to shift. We felt powerless. And after a long wrestle and with no other options within a broken system, we had to inform the court we could no longer look after Roscoe; it felt like a total tragedy. We'd desperately wanted to help this young man so affected by the soul-violation of severe trauma, but couldn't. Participating in his story and trying everything we could think of to help him was to no avail. But despite contending for a miracle, we didn't see one – or at least we haven't seen one yet.

I tell this story alongside the story of Simi's adoption, not to deter hope but rather to show that the outcome doesn't belong to us. It can be all too easy when looking at diagrams to think that if we follow them 'correctly', we'll see a certain result – that's our worldly success-wired brains talking again. The difficult truth is that putting ourselves in a position of risk and depending on God's deliverance, sticking our neck out, praying and believing, carries no guarantee or neat formula that will ensure we get the results we hope for. Life is rarely clear-cut. There is a mystery to God's activity in the world. Sometimes we see visible results, other times we don't. But this should never stop us trying. Unanswered questions, confusing delays, sadness or frustration – none of this precludes the power of God at work. The point is that *even when* God is active, he's not just working *for* us but working *in* us too. And as creator of the universe he is under no obligation to match our timescales or expectations.

The wider the gap between our hopes for another way and the fulfilment of his purposes, the greater the opportunity to lean into fellowship with Jesus' sufferings.

Glorious (un)success

Jesus lived the most fulfilling life any human possibly could, yet it was marked by suffering:

He was despised and rejected by mankind, a man of suffering, and familiar with pain.
(Isaiah 53:3)

During the days of Jesus' life on earth, he offered up prayers and petitions with fervent cries and tears to the one who could save him from death, and he was heard because of his reverent submission. Son though he was, he learned obedience from what he suffered.
(Hebrews 5:7–8)

Whether we say 'yes' to Jesus or reject him, suffering is part of life. Wouldn't you rather suffer *with* Jesus than *without* him? If you share your suffering with him you'll discover that he can redeem your pain – and this is a crucial factor in the spreading of the good news. As such, suffering is also a key to understanding joy. Those who have suffered most often end up carrying the deepest joy. This joy is not guaranteed, however – suffering can also make you bitter and sad. If Jesus learned obedience through what he suffered, there could surely be opportunity hidden in it for us too, couldn't there?

Suffering is deeply connected to glory.

And glory is a success of which the world knows nothing.

God's glory is described in Isaiah 6:3, where the heavenly host are singing 'Holy, holy, holy is the LORD Almighty; the whole earth is full of his glory'. God's glory is God's holiness on public display – the visible, discernible beauty of God's goodness and perfection.

And if suffering can ultimately mould us into the likeness of Jesus, then the public witness of his followers sanctified through hardship increases the glory of God. But Paul tells us that 'the minds of unbelievers' – those who haven't yet decided to follow Jesus – have been blinded from seeing 'the glory of Christ' (2 Corinthians 4:4) – which is why many won't understand the path of suffering and glory on to which God calls his followers.

In John 2:11 we're told that Jesus' turning water into wine 'was the first of the signs through which he revealed his glory; and his disciples believed in him'. The revealing of Jesus' glory led to the salvation of those who witnessed it. Above and beyond accolades, relevance, big numbers and big platforms, the way of Jesus followers is in a different direction completely, all of which can be summarised through what we've seen in this final chapter; it is 'to know Christ – yes, to know *the power of his resurrection* and *participation in his sufferings*' (Philippians 3:10).

When miracles are performed, they reveal God's glory. Power.

When suffering is redeemed, it reveals God's glory. Participation.

When they come together, people put their faith in him and are changed for ever.

Power and participation.

The way to (un)success.

Questions for reflection

1 What do you think of the terms 'revivalism' and 'activism'? Would you say you veer more towards one than the other? Which would you like to grow in, and how could you do that?
2 Can you relate to being not enough and being too much at the same time?
3 Do you have any personal prophetic words over your life? How might they inspire you to a systemically prophetic life?
4 Have you ever experienced God redeeming an area of suffering in your life?
5 Having read this chapter, do you view Philippians 3:10 any differently?

Love is our ultimate calling – love for God, love of self, love for others and love for the world ... There is no other adequate measure of success for us as Christians.
(Ruth Haley Barton[16])

Notes

Foreword

1 Thomas Merton, *New Seeds of Contemplation* (Boulder, CO: Shambhala, 2003), p. 113.

Introduction

1 James K. A. Smith, *You Are What You Love: The spiritual power of habit* (Grand Rapids, MI: Brazos Press, 2016), p. 11; emphasis original.

2 Dietrich Bonhoeffer, *Ethics*, ed. Eberhard Bethge, trans. Neville Horton Smith (London: SCM Press, 1955), p. 77.

3 James Mumford, *Vexed: Ethics beyond political tribes* (London: Bloomsbury Continuum, 2020), p. 75.

4 Paul Kingsnorth, 'The Cross and the Machine', *First Things*, June/July 2021; https://www.firstthings.com/article/2021/06/the-cross-and-the-machine (accessed 17 June 2023).

5 Kingsnorth, 'The Cross and the Machine'.

6 Smith, *You Are What You Love*, p. 2.

7 José Humphreys, *Seeing Jesus in East Harlem: What happens when churches show up and stay put* (Downers Grove, IL: InterVarsity Press, 2018), p. 34.

8 I'm having to stop myself writing in more detail about Manenberg because that's what my first book was about – have a read; it's called *No Neutral Ground: Finding Jesus in a Cape Town ghetto* (London: Hodder & Stoughton, 2019). If you like it, perhaps leave a nice review?

9 Look us up at www.treeoflife.org.za.

10 Smith, *You Are What You Love*, p. 22.

11 Smith, *You Are What You Love*, p. 20.

12 Smith, *You Are What You Love*, p. 21; emphasis original.

13 See 'Jesus is Most Historically Significant Person Ever, Claims New Book "Who is Bigger"', *Huffington Post*, 12 December 2013; https://

www.huffpost.com/entry/jesus-historically-significant_n_4420934 (accessed 17 June 2023).

1 Success is ... Following God's calling over good ideas

1 Ronald Rolheiser, *Sacred Fire* (New York: Image, 2014), p. 40.
2 Alasdair MacIntyre, *After Virtue: A study in moral theory*, 3rd edn (London: Bloomsbury Academic, 2007), p. 250.
3 Quoted in Jean M. Humez, *Harriet Tubman: The life and the life stories* (Madison, WI: University of Wisconsin Press, 2003), p. 261.
4 James K. A. Smith, *You Are What You Love: The spiritual power of habit* (Grand Rapids, MI: Brazos Press, 2016), p. 38.
5 Christopher L. Heuertz and Christine D. Pohl, *Friendship at the Margins: Discovering mutuality in service and mission* (Downers Grove, IL: InterVarsity Press, 2010), p. 19.
6 Hans Rosling, with Ola Rosling and Anna Rosling Rönnlund, *Factfulness: Ten reasons we're wrong about the world* (New York: Flatiron Books, 2018), p. 189.
7 Henri J. M. Nouwen, *The Return of the Prodigal Son: A story of homecoming* (New York: Doubleday, 1994), pp. 42–3.
8 John Wimber, *The Dynamics of Spiritual Growth* (London: Hodder & Stoughton, 1990), pp. 124–5.
9 Jackie Pullinger, 'The Testing of Your Faith', talk at International House of Prayer, Kansas City, 25 March 2018; https://www.youtube.com/watch?v=qGMoEy40nTM (accessed 17 June 2023).
10 Pullinger, 'The Testing of Your Faith'.
11 Eugene H. Peterson, *A Long Obedience in the Same Direction: Discipleship in an instant society* (Downers Grove, IL: InterVarsity Press, 2000), p. 166.
12 Peterson, *A Long Obedience*, p. 160.
13 This is where some of the commentators I read have in-depth discussions about the cultural customs at the time, regarding the potential danger faced by husbands and wives entering foreign lands – including the possibility that the wife would be raped and the husband killed. Hence, for some, Abram's rational pre-emptive decision to claim he and his wife were siblings may actually have

saved their lives. Honestly, I'm not sure. But what is fairly clear is that the story of Abram/Abraham, along with the 'man of faith' narrative we so often draw, also conveys to us a man with a fairly dark side who struggles with obeying God.

14 Heuertz and Pohl, *Friendship at the Margins*, p. 35.

15 St Augustine, *Confessions*, Book I.i, trans. R. S. Pine-Coffin (Harmondsworth: Penguin, 1961), p. 21.

16 Smith, *You Are What You Love*, p. 8; emphasis original.

17 Smith, *You Are What You Love*, p. 11.

2 Success is ... Pursuing relationship over relevance

1 Wendell Berry, 'The Unsettling of America', in *The Art of the Commonplace: The agrarian essays of Wendell Berry* (Berkeley, CA: Counterpoint, 2002), p. 39.

2 Jackie Pullinger, from a talk at Asbury Theological Seminary, Wilmore, Kentucky, October 1993.

3 Thomas Keating, *The Human Condition: Contemplation and transformation* (Mahwah, NJ: Paulist Press, 1999), p. 38.

4 Carrie Fisher, quoted in Amy Larocca, 'The Mentalist', *New York*, 24 Sept. 2009; https://nymag.com/arts/theater/features/59427/ (accessed 27 May 2023).

5 Henri J. M. Nouwen, *In the Name of Jesus: Reflections on Christian leadership* (New York: Crossroad, 1989), p. 16.

6 Many churches do great work feeding communities with no strings attached. I've sadly experienced food used as a manipulative tool to 'win converts' in poorer communities. It's highly problematic.

7 Nouwen, *In the Name of Jesus*, p. 73.

8 Nouwen, *In the Name of Jesus*, p. 73.

9 Christopher L. Heuertz and Christine D. Pohl, *Friendship at the Margins: Discovering mutuality in service and mission* (Downers Grove, IL: InterVarsity Press, 2010), p. 31.

10 'Coloured' is a local South African term, simply put, for those of mixed racial and cultural heritage.

11 Julian C. Adams, *Terra Nova: Fulfilling your call to redeem the earth and make all things new* (Boston, MA: Frequentsee, 2020), p. 34.

12 Adams, *Terra Nova*, p. 35.
13 Adams, *Terra Nova*, p. 36.
14 Nouwen, *In the Name of Jesus*, p. 17.
15 Nouwen, *In the Name of Jesus*, p. 17.
16 Richard Rohr, *Breathing Under Water: Spirituality and the twelve steps* (Cincinnati, OH: Franciscan Media, 2011), p. 2.
17 Nouwen, *In the Name of Jesus*, p. 32.
18 Nouwen, *In the Name of Jesus*, p. 20.
19 Whatever 'cultural Marxism' means – in my experience those who refer to it hardly ever have a clear understanding of what they mean but have heard it used by others as a way of shutting down debate. More on this in Chapter 5.
20 Nouwen, *In the Name of Jesus*, p. 21.
21 Nouwen, *In the Name of Jesus*, p. 23.
22 Nouwen, *In the Name of Jesus*, p. 24.
23 Nouwen, *In the Name of Jesus*, p. 25.
24 Nouwen, *In the Name of Jesus*, p. 34.
25 Nouwen, *In the Name of Jesus*, pp. 36–7.
26 Nouwen, *In the Name of Jesus*, p. 37.
27 Nouwen, *In the Name of Jesus*, p. 38.
28 Trevor Hudson, *Friendship With God: How God's offer of relationship can change your life* (Cape Town: Struik Christian Media, 2015), p. 125.
29 See, for example, 'The Millennial Friendship Crisis', World Economic Forum, 14 August 2019; https://www.weforum.org/agenda/2019/08/the-millennial-friendship-crisis/ (accessed 27 May 2023).
30 Hudson, *Friendship With God*, p. 126.
31 John Mark Comer, *The Ruthless Elimination of Hurry: How to stay emotionally healthy and spiritually alive in the chaos of the modern world* (London: Hodder & Stoughton, 2019).
32 Nouwen, *In the Name of Jesus*, p. 43.
33 Nouwen, *In the Name of Jesus*, p. 44.
34 Nouwen, *In the Name of Jesus*, p. 53.
35 Nouwen, *In the Name of Jesus*, p. 53.
36 Dietrich Bonhoeffer, *Ethics*, trans. Neville Horton Smith (New York: Touchstone, 1995), p. 78.

37 Clare Pretorius, sermon, Manenberg, December 2018.

38 Doreen Massey, *Space, Place and Gender* (Cambridge: Polity Press, 1994), p. 150.

39 T. J. Gorringe, *A Theology of the Built Environment: Justice, empowerment, redemption* (Cambridge: Cambridge University Press, 2002), p. 21.

40 Ruth Haley Barton, *Strengthening the Soul of Your Leadership: Seeking God in the crucible of ministry* (Downers Grove, IL: InterVarsity Press, 2008), p. 111; emphasis original.

41 David P. Leong, *Race and Place: How urban geography shapes the journey to reconciliation* (Downers Grove, IL: InterVarsity Press, 2017), p. 78.

42 Christopher Heuertz, *Unexpected Gifts: Discovering the way of community* (New York: Howard Books, 2013), p. 109.

43 Heuertz, *Unexpected Gifts*, p. 115.

44 Heuertz, *Unexpected Gifts*, p. 115.

45 Heuertz, *Unexpected Gifts*, p. 115.

46 Jackie Pullinger, 'The Testing of Your Faith', a talk at International House of Prayer, Kansas City, 25 March 2018; https://www.youtube.com/watch?v=qGMoEy40nTM (accessed 17 June 2023).

47 Heuertz and Pohl, *Friendship at the Margins*, p. 120.

48 Heuertz and Pohl, *Friendship at the Margins*, p. 122.

3 Success is ... Growing in depth over volume

1 Elias Chacour, quoted in Sam Wells, *Incarnational Mission: Being with the world* (Norwich: Canterbury Press, 2018), p. 220.

2 John Shelby Spong, *Eternal Life: A New Vision: Beyond religion, beyond theism, beyond heaven and hell* (New York: HarperOne, 2009), p. 119. While I don't agree with everything Bishop John Shelby Spong says, I find this quote helpful.

3 Francis Spufford, *Unapologetic: Why, despite everything, Christianity can still make surprising emotional sense* (London: Faber & Faber, 2012), p. 57.

4 The more I read that last sentence the more amazed I am this book was published!

5 N. T. Wright, *Surprised by Hope: Rethinking heaven, the resurrection and the mission of the church* (London: SPCK, 2007), p. 204.

6 James Baldwin, 'A Report from Occupied Territory', *The Nation*, 11 July 1966; https://www.thenation.com/article/culture/report-occupied-territory/ (accessed 29 May 2023).

7 C. S. Lewis, *The Screwtape Letters* (New York: HarperOne, 1996), p. 119.

8 Kyle Chayka, 'The Subway that Sunk: How Silicon Valley helps spread the same sterile aesthetic across the world', *The Verge*, 3 August 2016; https://www.theverge.com/2016/8/3/12325104/airbnb-aesthetic-global-minimalism-startup-gentrification (accessed 29 May 2023).

9 Carey Nieuwhof, '5 Faulty Assumptions about the Future Church' (undated); https://careynieuwhof.com/5-faulty-assumptions-about-the-future-church/ (accessed 17 June 2023).

10 John Inge, *A Christian Theology of Place* (Aldershot: Ashgate, 2003), p. 130.

11 Inge, *Christian Theology of Place*, p. 136.

12 Saskia Sassen, *Cities in a World Economy*, 2nd edn (London: Sage, 2000), p. 144.

13 Dallas Willard, 'Spirituality Made Hard', an interview with Mike Yaconelli, *The Door*, May/June 1993, no. 129; https://dwillard.org/articles/spirituality-made-hard (accessed 20 July 2022).

14 Willard, 'Spirituality Made Hard'.

15 There's a great meme of the actor Daniel Kaluuya's pose from the film *Get Out* (dir. Jordan Peele, Universal Pictures), a close-up of his shocked face, tears running down his cheeks, with the words: 'When you finally realise that the prosperity gospel offers you everything that Satan offered Jesus.'

16 Henri J. M. Nouwen, *Reaching Out: The three movements of the spiritual life* (New York: Doubleday, 1975), p. 36.

17 Henri J. M. Nouwen, *The Return of the Prodigal Son: A story of homecoming* (New York: Doubleday, 1994), p. 41.

18 Based on Philippians 2:5–11.

19 Russell Moore, 'The Upside-Down Church: Witnessing to a strange gospel', *Plough*, 13 October 2015; https://www.plough.com/en/topics/

faith/discipleship/upside-down-church?fbclid=IwAR2ySvHDNTq
u4U2lb4khMjozMKvp19QbOxWpMN-f1rbNRESEtBfdWRg3uR8
(accessed 29 May 2023).

20 G. K. Chesterton, 'The Spice of Life', *The Listener*, 18 March 1936, in
The Spice of Life and Other Essays, ed. Dorothy Collins (Beaconsfield:
Darwen Finlayson, 1964); http://www.gkc.org.uk/gkc/books/Spice_
Of_Life.html#spice (accessed 20 July 2022).

21 I think atheism might be one of my favourite 'first-world problems',
along with not being able to find the end of the sticky tape, having a
house too big for your wi-fi router, your swimming pool filter getting
clogged and not being able to find pine nuts at the deli. It's worth
saying that I've never met an atheist in Manenberg.

22 Chesterton, 'The Spice of Life'.

23 Chesterton, 'The Spice of Life'.

24 Gregory the Great, *Liber Regulae Pastoralis*, in *Nicene and Post-
Nicene Fathers, Second Series, Vol. 12: Leo the Great, Gregory the
Great*, ed. Philip Schaff and Henry Wace (Oxford: Parker, 1895),
p. 18; http://www.documentacatholicaomnia.eu/01p/0590-0604,_SS_
Gregorius_I_Magnus,_Regulae_Pastoralis_Liber_[Schaff],_EN.pdf
[p. 446] (accessed 29 May 2023).

25 Sure, the answer to 2+2 isn't 'empathy' etc. But I think the point is
fairly self-explanatory. If we were to prioritise empathy and kindness
as the primary forms of witness, we'd be on to a good thing.

26 Great caution is needed here. I don't want to end up using the
same means as the approach I'm questioning. More than that, I
don't want to suggest I have an issue with healthy accountability of
professional integrity. Even more than that, I believe that anyone
who courageously speaks up against those who've abused power – in
whatever way – must be listened to and taken seriously.

27 Two of my favourite suggestions on what Jesus may have written
are: he wrote the secret sins that each of the religious accusers were
themselves guilty of; or he wrote the name of everyone in the crowd,
from oldest to youngest, and as each saw their name they walked
away. Ultimately, who knows?

28 Wells, *Incarnational Mission*, p. 91.

29 Christena Cleveland differentiates between two different types of dispute. She defines 'realistic conflict' as fighting 'for an immutable truth', whereas a 'cultural threat' is simply 'a different perspective that threatens ours'. *Disunity in Christ: Uncovering the hidden forces that keep us apart* (Downers Grove, IL: InterVarsity Press, 2013), p. 139. While I don't agree with everything Cleveland says, and acknowledge she's adopted some strong postures subsequent to this work, I find this research on reconciliation insightful.

30 Cleveland, *Disunity in Christ*, p. 146.

31 Cleveland, *Disunity in Christ*, p. 147.

32 Cleveland, *Disunity in Christ*, p. 156.

33 Tyler Staton, *Praying Like Monks, Living Like Fools: An invitation to the wonder and mystery of prayer* (Grand Rapids, MI: Zondervan, 2022), p. 83.

4 Success is … Transforming over transferring

1 Dr Glenn Doyle, @DrDoyleSays, Twitter post, 7 October 2020.

2 C. S. Lewis, *The Great Divorce* (New York: HarperCollins, 2001), p. viii.

3 James Baldwin, 'Notes of a Native Son', in *Collected Essays* (New York: Library of America, 1998), p. 75.

4 For more on how trauma affects the mind and body, see Bessel van der Kolk, *The Body Keeps the Score: Mind, brain and body in the transformation of trauma* (London: Penguin, 2015).

5 Aaron White, *Recovering: From brokenness and addiction to blessedness and community* (Grand Rapids, MI: Baker Academic, 2020), p. 13.

6 Arthur C. Brooks, *From Strength to Strength: Finding success, happiness and deep purpose in the second half of life* (London: Bloomsbury, 2022), p. 50.

7 Anna Lembke, *Dopamine Nation: Finding balance in the age of indulgence* (New York: Dutton, 2021), p. 1.

8 See, for example, Christophe Haubursin, 'It's Not You. Phones are Designed to be Addicting: The three design elements that make smartphones so hard to put down', *Vox*, 27 February 2018; https://www.vox.com/2018/2/27/17053758/phone-addictive-design-google-apple (accessed 17 June 2023).

9 Lembke, *Dopamine Nation*, p. 3.

10 White, *Recovering*, p. 16.

11 Erin Khar, *Strung Out: One last hit and other lies that nearly killed me* (New York: Park Row, 2020); quoted from 'Heroin, Crystal Meth and Motherhood: Confessions of a privileged drug addict', *The Times*, 10 October 2020; https://www.thetimes.co.uk/article/heroin-crystal-meth-and-motherhood-confessions-of-a-privileged-drug-addict-hj005zpml (accessed 25 July 2022).

12 Shaun Shelly, 'Bringing in the Army Turns People on the Cape Flats into Targets', *Daily Maverick*, 23 July 2019; https://www.dailymaverick.co.za/article/2019-07-23-bringing-in-the-army-turns-people-on-the-cape-flats-into-targets/ (accessed 17 June 2023).

13 White, *Recovering*, p. 18.

14 Resmaa Menakem, quoted on @OnBeing, Twitter feed, 6 June 2020.

15 I know, right? But I'd prefer not to say who this was.

16 José Humphreys, *Seeing Jesus in East Harlem: What happens when churches show up and stay put* (Downers Grove, IL: InterVarsity Press, 2018), p. 17.

17 Humphreys, *Seeing Jesus in East Harlem*, p. 21.

18 Humphreys, *Seeing Jesus in East Harlem*, p. 21.

19 Humphreys, *Seeing Jesus in East Harlem*, p. 22.

20 White, *Recovering*, p. 13.

21 van der Kolk, *The Body Keeps the Score*, p. 13.

22 See TRE's site, www.traumaprevention.com (accessed 30 May 2023).

5 Success is ... Being a faithful presence in the culture wars

1 Barbara Brown Taylor, 'The Perfect Mirror', *The Christian Century* 115:9 (March 18–25, 1998), p. 283; https://www.religion-online.org/article/the-perfect-mirror-jn-181-1937/ (accessed 1 June 2023).

2 Emil Brunner, *Man in Revolt: A Christian anthropology* (first published in German, 1939), trans. Olive Wyon (Cambridge: Lutterworth Press, 1957), p. 34.

3 David Brooks, *The Second Mountain: The quest for a moral life* (New York: Random House, 2019), p. 4.

4 Brooks, *The Second Mountain*, p. 4.

5 Eugene H. Peterson, *A Long Obedience in the Same Direction: Discipleship in an instant society* (Downers Grove, IL: InterVarsity Press, 2000), p. 25.

6 Brooks, *The Second Mountain*, p. 34.

7 Brooks, *The Second Mountain*, p. 35.

8 Brooks, *The Second Mountain*, p. 35.

9 At least to play our part in it – no one can do all of that! Also, whereas *equality* has to do with giving everyone the exact same resources, *equity* involves distributing resources based on the needs. The kingdom of God is less about equality and more about equity – Jesus put first those the world put last.

10 N. T. Wright, *Surprised by Hope: Rethinking heaven, the resurrection and the mission of the church* (London: SPCK, 2007), p. 277.

11 Elizabeth Phillips, *Political Theology: A guide for the perplexed* (London: T&T Clark International, 2012), p. 4.

12 Quoted in David J. Bosch, *Transforming Mission: Paradigm shifts in theology of mission* 20th anniversary edn (Maryknoll, NY: Orbis Books, 2011), p. 386.

13 C. S. Lewis, *Mere Christianity* (London: Bles, 1952; HarperCollins, 2002), p. 128.

14 Meg Jay, *The Defining Decade: Why your twenties matter and how to make the most of them now* (New York: Twelve, 2012), p. 6; Jay (p. 207) attributes the term to the sociologist James Côté.

15 Brooks, *The Second Mountain*, p. 18.

16 Brooks, *The Second Mountain*, p. 19.

17 Martin Luther King, Jr., *Strength to Love* (Boston, MA: Beacon Press, 1963, 1981), p. 1.

18 King, *Strength to Love*, p. 1

19 King, *Strength to Love*, p. 2.

20 King, *Strength to Love*, p. 3.

21 King, *Strength to Love*, p. 4.

22 King, *Strength to Love*, p. 5.

23 King, *Strength to Love*, p. 6.

24 King, *Strength to Love*, p. 7.

25 King, *Strength to Love*, p. 8.

26 Sam Wells, *Incarnational Mission: Being with the world* (Norwich: Canterbury Press, 2018), p. 201.

27 Walter Brueggemann, *The Prophetic Imagination*, 2nd edn (Minneapolis, MN: Augsburg Fortress, 2001), p. 3.

28 Brueggemann, *The Prophetic Imagination*, p. 86.

29 Wright, *Surprised by Hope*, p. 25.

30 Wright, *Surprised by Hope*, p. 26.

31 Wright, *Surprised by Hope*, p. 26.

32 Wright, *Surprised by Hope*, p. 5; emphasis original.

33 Wright, *Surprised by Hope*, p. 211.

34 Wright, *Surprised by Hope*, p. 211.

35 Wright, *Surprised by Hope*, p. 213; emphasis original.

36 Anand Giridharadas, *Winners Take All: The elite charade of changing the world* (New York: Knopf, 2018), pp. 4–5.

37 Fun fact: the word 'oxymoron' is itself an oxymoron! In Greek, *oxy* means 'wise' and *moros* means 'foolish'.

38 Stanley Hauerwas and Romand Coles, *Christianity, Democracy, and the Radical Ordinary: Conversations between a radical democrat and a Christian* (Eugene, OR: Cascade Books, 2008) p. 3.

39 Alasdair MacIntyre, 'A Partial Response to my Critics', in *After MacIntyre: Critical perspectives on the work of Alasdair MacIntyre*, ed. John Horton and Susan Mendus (Notre Dame, IN: University of Notre Dame Press, 1994), p. 303.

40 Edward Abbey, 'The Second Rape of the West', in *The Journey Home: Some words in defense of the American West* (New York: Plume, 1991), p. 183; emphasis original.

41 Vinoth Ramachandra, *Sarah's Laughter: Doubt, tears and Christian hope* (Carlisle: Langham Global Library, 2020), p. 58.

6 Success is ... Living in power and participation

1 Jason Upton, 'A Hammer and an Awkward Nail'. Songwriter Jason Upton, Publisher Key of David Music, copyright © 2012 Key of David Music (adm at IntegratedRights.com). CCLI number 7085088.

2 Rob Reimer, *Spiritual Authority: Partnering with God to release the kingdom* (Franklin, TN: Carpenter's Son Publishing, 2020).

3 Archbishop Lazar Puhalo, *Freedom to Believe: Personhood and freedom in Orthodox Christian ontology* (Dewdney, BC: Synaxis Press, 2017), p. 176.

4 Generally attributed to A. W. Tozer.

5 Alan Scott, *Scattered Servants: Unleashing the church to bring life to the city* (Colorado Springs, CO: David C. Cook, 2018), pp. 182–3.

6 Scott, *Scattered Servants*, p. 187.

7 'How Load Shedding is Tearing Through South Africa', *BusinessTech*, 21 September 2022; https://businesstech.co.za/news/business/627280/how-load-shedding-is-tearing-through-south-africas-economy/#:~:text=There's%20the%20cost%20of%20downtime,costs%20also%20escalate%2C%20he%20said (accessed 16 February 2023).

8 'Stage 6 Load Shedding Costs South Africa R900 Million a Day', *BusinessTech*, 6 February 2023; https://businesstech.co.za/news/energy/662515/stage-6-load-shedding-costs-south-africa-r900-million-a-day-sarb/ (accessed 16 February 2023).

9 I promise I'm not making this up! See 'Eskom Blames Rain, Wet Coal for Generation Capacity Failures', *Eyewitness News*; https://ewn.co.za/2022/04/19/eskom-blames-rain-wet-coal-for-generation-capacity-failures (accessed 17 June 2023).

10 Elisabeth Kübler-Ross, *Death: The final stage of growth* (New York: Touchstone, 1986), p. 96.

11 Viktor E. Frankl, *Man's Search for Meaning* (London: Penguin, 2004), p. 12.

12 Jackie Pullinger, 'Go'; https://www.youtube.com/watch?v=iIc631LALz8 (accessed 16 February 2023).

13 C. S. Lewis, *Mere Christianity* (London: Fount, 1981), p. 127.

14 Thomas Merton, 'September 1968 Circular Letter to Friends', in *The Asian Journal of Thomas Merton*, ed. Naomi Burton, Brother Patrick Hart and James Laughlin (New York: New Directions, 1975), p. 296.

15 N. T. Wright, *Surprised by Hope: Rethinking heaven, the resurrection and the mission of the church* (London: SPCK, 2007), p. 264.

16 Ruth Haley Barton, *Pursuing God's Will Together: A discernment practice for leadership groups* (Westmont, IL: InterVarsity Press, 2012), p. 55.

🌀 **24-7 PRAYER**

H O W   T O   B E

(un)successful

A free small group series designed
to accompany Pete Portal's book,
How to be (Un)Successful

———— FEATURING ————

Six video sessions with Pete Portal and friends

Discussion guides for each session to help you and
your community to go deeper together

Launching Autumn 2023

24-7prayer.com/unsuccessful

Milton Keynes UK
Ingram Content Group UK Ltd.
UKHW020629231123
433120UK00014B/303